ENDORSEMENTS

"Having worked with Small to Mid-sized Business Owners over the last 40 + years I have found that most have spent all their time working on how to get into the Business and not on how to get out of it. This Book is a MUST READ for every Business Owner out there. The writers experience is well defined in each chapter & page."

Mike Reinhart
Financial Advisor and Founder
Global Wealth Solutions

"Entrepreneurs and business owners are often so engrossed in the day to day activities of the business they neglect the "end game". The information provided within should assist to get that thought process underway and lead to an outcome that is more than just a dream. An easy to read book that highlights aspects of business that is often overlooked should be on every owners desk!"

Len Rhoades
Financial Advisor
Global Wealth Solutions

"Jamie's experience, knowledge and sincere desire to create Estate Plans tailored to a client's unique requirements and desires is refreshing! I know that when Jamie is involved with the strategic planning, a client's desired result will be successfully achieved. I have trusted Jamie with my personal Estate Plan and feel confident that he will exceed the expectations of those that choose to engage his services."

Paul Hix
Financial Advisor
Edward Jones Financial

"Jamie and Randall are consummate professionals who guide business owners through the creation, growth and sharing of their business and life skills and wisdom."

Richard Kerbawy
JD Managing Partner
Wilson, Lett & Kerbawy

"This book is an excellent introduction to the art of preserving and protecting the wealth you've worked your entire life to create. Moore and Borkus explain how to maximize your life's work using real world examples that are easily understood. This is truly a great book."

Thomas Kalil
Attorney

SELL OR TRANSFER YOUR BUSINESS

James L. Moore, JD; CExP
RANDALL H. BORKUS, MS, JD, LL.M. TAX, CEPA

Borkuslaw Group, Ltd.
1415 West 22nd Street
Tower Floor
Oak Brook, IL 60523

Law Offices of James L. Moore
4595 Broadmoor Ave., SE
Suite 295
Grand Rapids, MI 49512

Design and layout by Zine (www.zinegraphics.com)

Library of Congress Number: 2024916072

ISBN: 978-1-944887-91-9
digital ISBN: 978-1-944887-92-6

DEDICATION

For my incredible wife and life's journey partner, Jan, who has enabled me to appreciate, in our shared labor and adventure, the force of St. Augustine's remark that "a friend is someone with whom one may dare to share the counsel of one's heart," and without whom I would not be the man, husband, father and grandfather that I am and continue to aspire to be. You truly are "my special angel."

Jamie L. Moore

I dedicate this book to my wonderful wife, Janis Borkus, and my stepdaughter, Melissa Nava, for their support, encouragement and their patience with my dedication to long days and my persistent nature to always push myself to be better.

Randall H. Borkus

TABLE OF CONTENTS

FOREWORD

by Ben Glass

Fairfax, Virginia

Attorney, Coach and (most importantly) Dad to 9

You Built It. Now What?

Business owners and entrepreneurs are a special breed. We are built to create. We have more creative ideas in a day then most people have in a year. We see most every challenge as an opportunity to solve a problem, often in a new way. Many of us have built one (or more) businesses that have provided a lifestyle and income that has allowed us to live the life we want to live. We have a mindset of abundance.

Know what we aren't very good at? Looking at the end game. Giving up the baby we built. Handing over the reigns to someone else. Taking it easy. Watching others now work as hard as we did all those years, while we take a break, or move on to a new venture.

Know what we don't have a lot of experience doing? Selling or transferring our businesses when we are done with them. Doesn't happen all that often. We don't even know what questions to ask, let alone what the right answers might be to those questions.

Jamie Moore is a great lawyer with a ton of experience. But, truth be told, knowing how to "dot I's and cross T's" is only part of what lawyers like Jamie do.

Jamie's really a business guru. You know what the top guru's do? The very best in the world? They get people like you and me to sit down, quiet our brains and think about the future. Not just any future, but the future that would really be perfect for us. Thought leaders like Jamie force people like us to ask ourselves really hard and serious questions.

Sell or Transfer Your Business is the book that will not only provoke the right questions but will help you get to the right answer for you and your family. Jamie's going to ask you: "what would be perfect for you?" Start thinking about that.

This book is great for another reason too. It's filled with great business ideas. This book will be most valuable to someone who is years away from selling the business they built. Every business should be "built to sell" because one way or another its going to be sold or transferred!

And one more thing: thanks for being an entrepreneur. You are the engine that runs the world!

FOREWORD

by Kevin J. Imhoff

Investment Advisor and Financial Planner since 1985
Owner of Blue Diamond Financial Solutions and
Blue Diamond Financial Coaching

I have helped thousands of families and small business owners navigate through the financial challenges each lifecycle families face and unique complexities that come with owning and running a business.

My one key question for you, "Upon your death, will your family bless or curse your name on how you left them financially?"

As a Financial Planner I have seen the pain of grief that comes with the loss of a loved one from a financial perspective that few ever see. The difference in grief between those loved whose financial house is "in order" and those loved ones whose financial house is a mess are polar opposites.

One family reflects on the memories, impact, and joy the decease brought to the family. The sadness, pain, and grief are there but there is a future.

The family's finances that are a "mess" are overwhelmed with fear and panic. Their focus is on the immediate. Constant worry and pressure hit them. "Where is the money going to come from to pay the bills? Will I have to go back to work? Will the cars be repossessed? Will we lose our home? How will we ever get through this?

Those deceased loved ones that own a business are 100 X more complex. As a business owner reading this book, you know what I mean without going into details. Again, the difference between the grief of the families of those who planned and prepared and those who did not are on opposites sides of the universe.

The authors of this book are gifts from God that bring systems and solutions you know you need. Take action now. Contact the authors and start the process to give one of the greatest gifts you can leave to your family, a financial house “in order” and a written plan for your business transition.

For those that just thought, I have time… I will get around to it… There is no rush…

Allow me to introduce a close friend of mine I’ve known for 30+ years. He owns a very successful roofing, siding, window replacement business. He’s charismatic, he’s everybody’s friend, a great salesman, can do the install work, his wife does all the business admin, his two sons work with him, truly a family business. As I sit and type this forward, less than 10 days ago, he started his work week just like every other week. He and his wife went to a job site to clean up and give the homeowners their final bill. As they were working his wife noticed something was off on how he was moving. My friend had a mild headache and noticed his left hand wasn’t “working” quite right.

His wife thought he may be having a stroke, so she drove him to the emergency room, and this is what happened next. The hospital ran a CAT Scan and discovered a 2" size tumor on the front side of his brain. Two days later, on his 57th birthday, he had brain surgery. The doctor was able to remove 80% of the tumor. Lab results of the tumor were done and came back with bad news. The doctor came in, recapped the surgery, and revealed he has Stage 4 brain cancer. I'm numb just reliving this. He has scheduled a second "opinion" review at a major hospital in Ann Arbor and starting consultation with an oncologist on a cancer treatment strategy. My friend's days are numbered. He thought he had time. He doesn't. Suddenly the circumstances of facing his mortality and urgency to get his estate, his finances and his business in order are real. Don't wait…

The questions Jamie asks in each chapter are brilliant! Every business owner no matter what stage their business is in can benefit from investing time to reflect on and answer truthfully each and every question he asks. Being reminded, what was the purpose of starting, building, rebuilding, reframing, redirecting, and growing our businesses is critical in how we customize our strategies for transitioning our lives as business owners for the next stage of our lives.

Each Chapter is filled with "nuggets of truth and wisdom", enjoy the process of discovering those "nuggets" that will directly impact your decision-making process on your journey of getting your succession plan in place.

I respect Jamie's faith, love of God, family, and Country. His example and lifelong pursuit of continually learning, self-improvement, remaining relevant and impactful are admirable. I appreciate his writing style in his newest book. I felt he was talking to me verses talking at me or over my head in legalize while addressing the complexities of Selling or Transferring ones business.

Randal's contribution was a reminder that there is always another level of excellence and expertise in business planning and consulting. Randal has the wisdom and experience to ask the right questions of family business owners then create multiple layers of solutions to protect our loved ones from predators, creditors, and the overreaching burdensome IRS.

ABOUT THE AUTHOR

James L. Moore, JD, CExP

James L. Moore, JD, Counselor at Law, principle and founder of The Law Offices of James L. Moore, PC is known as the "expert's-expert". Moore's reputation as a practical problem solver and bottom line communicator provides an environment which allows him to connect with the audience due to his extensive personal, legal, and practical business experience. Moore has 30 years of experience as an estate planning, business succession and tax attorney helping hundreds of clients plan for, protect, and preserve their personal estates and businesses. Moore's focus provides a proven system that allows individuals and business owners to pass along their wisdom and legacy values with their wealth and business.

As a Senior Contributing Fellow with the National Network of Estate Planning Attorneys and a former member of the National Advisory Council of the US Small Business Administration appointed by then President Ronald Regan, Moore is a sought after speaker and legal strategist. He has spoken to groups of tax, legal, financial, and other business professionals ranging from small business owner retreats to 5,000 participant weekend personal development seminars.

Moore obtained his Juris Doctorate after the completion of a tour of duty in Vietnam as a Marine Corp infantry officer. Since then, he has added to his professional education by obtaining the Advanced Estate and Business Succession Planning designation through the National Network of Estate Planning Attorneys. Moore has also earned the CExP designation (Certified Exit Planning Professional) from the Business Enterprise Institute and was recently selected by the State Bar of Michigan as a "Master Lawyer".

ABOUT THE AUTHOR

Randall H. Borkus, MS, JD, LL.M. Tax, CEPA

Attorney Randall H. Borkus' family comes from a long line of dairy farmers from Ladysmith, Wisconsin. After years of dairy market struggles Randall's grandfather Henry moved the family south to seek work and opportunity. Unfortunately, the Borkus family farm did not survive for a lack of guidance and planning.

This family history has fueled Randall's passion to dedicate his life's work to helping families preserve their bloodlines, their land, and their legacies.

For the past 19 years Randall has assisted hundreds of farm and ranch families in Illinois, Nebraska, North Dakota, Wyoming, and throughout the Midwest.

When it comes to preserving family legacies and bloodlines traditional estate planning simply doesn't fit for most farmers, ranchers and landowners. Keeping a farm or ranch in the family requires understanding family dynamics coupled with the implementation of unique customized planning strategies. These are not taught in schools and are the result of years of experience. Because of the complex nature of farmer, rancher and landowner estates, traditional planning approaches simply fall short.

Farming and ranching life is unique, and like no other lifestyle has its own distinctive value system that is deep and immovable. Farming and ranching family values are tough and deeply rooted in tradition and dedication. It is equally as tough to pass the operations on to the next generation and maintain the family heritage and bloodline preservation which is so vital to all farming and ranching families.

Randall's firm has a unique approach to bloodline preservation planning designed to keep the farm and ranch in the family.

INTRODUCTION

Don't be afraid for I am with you.
Don't be discouraged for I am your God.
I will strengthen you and help you.
I will hold you up with my victorious hand.
ISAIAH 41:10

Leaving your business and transferring ownership is likely the most significant financial transaction of your life. Nothing you do – in or out of your business – has greater financial and emotional consequences, and nothing less than the future quality of your life depends upon how well you manage the process.

How, then, do you prepare for the event that is the measure of your life's work? I am blessed to be a member of the Business enterprise Institute which has created through its members, many thousands of exit plans. We have found that most entrepreneurial owners are woefully unprepared to exit their businesses. As a consequence of poor or no preparation, these owners cannot leave when they want, with the money they need, and/or to the person they choose. There are many reasons for that lack of preparation, but once you read this book, the lack of information won't be the one that you can cite.

CHALLENGES

You face a number of challenges in your quest to leave your business on your terms. Some of these challenges may be apparent to you; many likely are not. Here are some of the ones you may not have anticipated:

- **Your Own Misperceptions.** Typically, owners and their businesses are far less prepared for a successful transition or exit than they may believe. The consequences of this misperception is more often than not complacency and inaction. A better consequence of seeing through these misperceptions is a focus on accelerating growth in the business value and cash flow by beginning to implement your transition or exit strategy now, before either burnout or boredom prevents you from taking the necessary actions.
- **A Lack of Resources.** Who or where can owners turn for help? Most advisors have not pursued the additional training necessary to help you develop and create a plan to successfully transition or exit your business. Most advisors, like most owners, have at best limited experience in planning much less orchestrating successful business transitions or exits. As a result, owners and their advisors don't know where to start, what to do, who can help, or what design principles to apply or options exist to achieve your goals.
- **Adequate time.** I can almost guarantee that it will take far longer to prepare and implement your successful transition or exit strategy than you might expect.

BENEFITS

Like the challenges you'll face in creating a transition or exit, some of the benefits of this planning are obvious and some are less so.

The three most obvious benefits are embedded in the title of this book: creating a legacy and leaving behind the successor owner you've chosen, on the date you have picked, with enough money in your bank account to satisfy your financial needs and wants for the rest of your life. Other benefits of this type of planning include:

» **Clears up the misperceptions.** In dispelling misperceptions about what it takes to transition or exit successfully, planning clears the path and creates a pathway or roadmap that achieves all of your goals and aspirations. In addition to the date, successor, an amount of cash you want, many, and probably most, owners set additional goals for themselves and for their businesses. These "values-based" goals may include: maintaining your legacy or the culture you've created within the business, continue to benefit the community, and many more.

» **Keeps owners in control.** A good transition or exit plan design should keep you in control of your business and of the course of your exit until you achieve all the goals you have for yourself, your family and your business.

» **Time to enjoy the ride.** While it will likely take several years perhaps to create a business that you can transfer in a way that achieves all of your goals, we will help you do so in a way that reduces the time you'll spend working in your business. Good transition or exit plans free up the demands of your time and transform the time you do spend in the business to time spent doing only things you want to do, not have to do.

THE ROAD AHEAD

Planning a transition or exit is similar to taking a journey accept this journey determines the quality of the rest of your life. Your exit has a beginning as well as a choice of which path to take from your start to your destination.

» **In Part I,** you will learn how to think about who, when, why, and how to transition or exit.

» **In Part II,** we will talk about how to add some horsepower to the vehicle that is going to take you to your finish line. Most of us need to increase the value of our companies and we will talk about these value drivers.

» **In Part III,** we will look at the eight Deal Killers that can knock your transition or exit plan off the track.

» **In Part IV,** we will examine all of the various tools, techniques, and legacy planning strategies to plan for and protect the legacy of your farm/ranch or business.

If one of your advisors gave you this book to read it is likely that he or she is familiar with the Seven-Step Exit Planning Process™ created by the Business Enterprise Institute. In executing the seven steps, thousands of owners have exited or transitioned from their company successfully so I have adhered to that process in this book:

SORRY! WE ARE NOT ALLOWED TO GIVE LEGAL ADVICE IN THIS BOOK.

We know the ins and outs of transition or exit planning for businesses. And so should you even before you start to leave your business.
You may find it interesting for example, that when you started your business, you also started to create a plan to exit your business.

Surprised? Don't be. All business owners leave their business eventually, one way or another, to family, employees, third parties, through liquidation, or "carried out on their shields." The overarching principle or point of this book is the way your transition or exit is organized and systemized now is crucial to making sure you exit "in style". That is, maximum money, minimum taxes, and zero hassles and messes!

This publication contains the opinions and ideas of the authors. It is intended to provide helpful and informative material on the subject addressed. The strategies outlined in this book may not be suitable for every individual, and are not guaranteed or warranted to produce any particular results.

This book is sold with the understanding that neither the author nor the publisher is engaged in rendering legal, financial, accounting, or

PART I

PLANNING YOUR TRANSITION OR EXIT

CHAPTER ONE

WHAT DO I WANT? WHAT DO I HAVE? WHAT ARE THE ROADBLOCKS?

"The beginning is the most important part of the work."
PLATO

Successful transition or exit planning requires you to carefully describe your goals and aspirations. Grading specific exit goals is essential to your ability to obtain the results you want. Knowing your goals precisely allows you to determine what, precisely, you need to do to achieve them. This is the topic of Part I.

Understanding the true value of your existing business and personal resources is likewise vital. It is that accurate understanding that establishes your starting point – what you have today to help achieve your goals. The difference between what you have today, what you want, and the resources you need to achieve your goals is your "gap".

What Exactly is a Transition or Exit Planning Strategy?

A transition or exit planning strategy is more than a way to just get rid of your business. That would simply be an exit. An exit or transition planning strategy is just that. A well-designed roadmap that considers and incorporates both the condition of your company now and where you expected to be in the future as well as your personal goals now and in the future. It serves kind of like an insurance policy so that when the time comes, you are in control of when, where, to whom, and for how much you can "sell" your business.

Let's talk just a minute about what we mean by "sell". Every single business existing today will eventually be sold or liquidated at some point in the future. Here's what we mean by "sold". Businesses may pass to the next generation (transition/succession). Businesses can be sold to a third party. Businesses can even be sold to their present owners when they decide to hold onto them for cash flow as investments rather than selling to free up the capital captured in the business. Businesses are sold to key employees (another form of transition/succession). Businesses that do not fall into one of these categories at some point generally get liquidated. Either go bankrupt, go out of business, or the assets are sold off.

The point is, you, as the business owner or manager, must plan for the inevitable sale of your business. What a great word "inevitability." In other words, to transition or exit successfully it's crucial to have a written Roadmap clearly defining your transition or exit strategy.

There is a reason the first thing they teach you on an airplane is how to use the oxygen mask by putting your own mask on first and then helping others around you and of course where are the exits.

Who Needs a Transition or Exit Strategy?

"Setting a goal is not the main thing.
It's deciding how you will go about achieving
it and staying with that plan."
TOM LANDRY

Anyone who owns a business or who contemplates owning a business needs a transition or exit strategy. So, listening to Coach Landry it is more important to know how you're going to get out then it is to know how to get into a business. Sometimes it's very easy to get in – most often somebody just writes a check. However, it's usually not so easy to get out. Ideally, someone writes another check to buy the ownership interest from the owner. That is, if he has in fact decided to sell.

However, what if the exit is unplanned? Death, disability, divorce, Government regulation overreaching, a bad economy, unexpected events and catastrophes, all create not only unexpected but more often usually unplanned exits.

For example, what if the person who is exiting is not the only owner? Who will buy the ownership interest and on what terms and conditions?

What happens to the business itself? Can the business even afford to buy out the owner? Who will run the business? What with the future course of the actual business itself be?

What will happen to the capitalization cash flow and taxes of the business? Will the unexpected exit cause a default in the underlying funding and capitalization of the company and require that for example, any and all loans must be paid off?

Is there any kind of a business continuity plan in place that will guide those now in charge, on not only how the business operates day-to-day but what is the owner's intention about to whom it should go?

To quote my original property law and contracts professor from law school many years ago "if it ain't in writing-- it ain't real!"

It is our belief and experience that if you don't have a well-designed written roadmap that addresses each and every one of these issues and the other issues that follow in this book you will have what we call the "no exit-exit".

Every transition or exit plan is owner-centric. Or, should be. Every action described in a transition or exit plan and taken by you, your employees and your advisors should have one purpose and one purpose only: achieving your goals.

How Will You Transition or Exit?

"When a man does not know what harbor he is heading for no wind is the right wind."
SENECA

As earlier stated, all businesses are ultimately sold, one way or another. As far as I understand five out of five people will die. No business owner will live forever so every business eventually gets sold.

As more fully explained in the white paper created by the Business Enterprise Institute; "Inevitabilities", there are a number of options available. This will be more fully explored in Part II. briefly, one way is through family succession such as a transition to the next generation. A second method would be a sale to a key employee or a"KEG" key employee group. Included in this method are a variety of tools and techniques including stock options, stock bonuses, and perhaps even an employee stock ownership plan ESOP.

The third method is the one most business owners instinctively think about which involves the sale to a third person or entity. More often than not this does not turn out to be the case due to market factors, financing, the nature of your business, and other factors. Moreover, this type of sale requires the most preparation because before the sale the third party will examine the business with something called "due diligence" that will be much more rigorous and intrusive than someone already familiar with the business who is acquiring it through a family succession for example. Also, a third-party sale means that the business will be and required to be especially prepared and positioned for this type of sale. This type of preparation takes time, even a couple of years in order to be successful.

The final method of sale is the saddest and messiest because the owners get little or no compensation at all for the business they work so hard to build. If no buyer can be obtained, or created, the business may be forced to either liquidate or, at worst, file bankruptcy. This sometimes results in the business owner not receiving anything for the stock or assets that are liquidated because those funds are used to cover the liabilities owed.

When Does a Transition or Exit Strategy Make Sense?

"For all your days prepare, and meet them ever alike; when you are the anvil, bear; when you are the hammer, strike."
EDWIN MARKHAM

ONE OWNER'S EXPERIENCE

In the past we worked with two business owners I'll call Tom and Jerry, who, years earlier, had started their own company.

As Time went on, Tom and Jerry continued to perform the same tasks they always had. Tom did not engage Jerry in any strategic planning, sales, office management, or the development of customer relationships. Jerry ran the service and field operations. When Jerry began to take frequent and extended vacations, arrive late and leave early, and using the company expense account quite liberally for personal expenses, Tom called me.

When we sat down to discuss his frustration, Tom told me that he had planned, in the absence of a buy/sell agreement, to try to terminate Jerry's ownership and begin the unpleasant process of negotiating a buyout. I suggested rather that he first sit down with Jerry to discuss his displeasure. Tom did meet with Jerry, and what he learned at the meeting made all the difference. Jerry readily admitted that he was pushing the envelope regarding "partner privilege" because he had so little to say in the rest of the business. Even though they were partners, Ton continued to make all the important decisions without consulting, or often even informing him. Since Jerry had no control over often distributions, major capital purchases, or the operation and future of the business, he decided to behave as a partner in the only way he knew how – by taking advantage of his special status.

As a result of that meeting, Tom and Jerry made two major decisions. First, they agreed to revisit and redefine their owner job descriptions and meet regularly to make major decisions. In essence, Tom and Jerry recognized and acknowledged that both of them had demonstrated their ability to contribute to the growth of the company so it was time to shift ownership responsibilities to him as well.

Tom's new job description left him the responsibility for relationships with the key customers and financial planning, which were vital to the growth of the business that require little in the way of day-to-day activity. Jerry assumed all the duties of daily operations and direct responsibility for all the income statements and expense items. Secondly, as part of this exercise, we also utilized the Business Enterprise Institute Seven Step Exit Planning Process™ to work out the conditions of ownership currently, and to put in place a written transition/exit plan into the future. This dramatically helped both owners realize that the term "partner" was more than just a title but in fact a structure and methodology we could use to actually create a written roadmap for the eventual transition of the business for everyone's benefit.

The bottom line was obviously that a well-planned transition or exit strategy was the answer to this dilemma. These strategies should always deal with what happens next with a business. The strategy could be a sale, it could be closing the business it could be growing the business it could be expanding the in planning systems and strategies to make the business better. Done well, a transition or exit strategy is a combination of various strategies crafted by a team of professionals – including the business owners – to fit a particular situation.

Why Do You Need a Transition or Exit Strategy?

Alice was a little startled by seeing the Cheshire
Sitting on a bolivar tree a few yards off.
"Cheshire" she began rather timidly, "would you
please tell me which way I ought to go from here?"
"That depends a good deal on where you want to get to,"
said the cat. "I don't much care where" said Alice. "Then it
doesn't matter which way you go," said the cat.
ALICE'S ADVENTURES IN WONDERLAND
BY LEWIS CARROLL

The second quote I'd like to offer you with this thought in mind, comes from one of my favorite philosophers the 1960s New York Yankees catcher Yogi Berra, "you have to be awful careful if you don't know where you're going because you might not get there."

In many meetings with new business owners just starting to plan how to begin and designed their new business, I often make the statement that it's more important to know how you're going to get out of this business that it is to decide how to get into this business. The new business owner may look at me quizzically or curiously but as we talk they begin to understand and eventually agree.

You probably know why you want to get into business. Maybe you have a passion for a particular thing and you want to develop a business around it. Maybe you want to develop your own business to provide income instead of having a job. Maybe you see a need in the marketplace that you want to service. You may want to build equity in a business or invest in real estate.

So, it is suggested to you that you design a business plan of some fashion that normally includes a beginning, how to operate during the life of the business and an ending. Getting started is usually pretty easy. Form an entity, open a bank account, get a tax ID number, put in some money, and away you go. Obviously without an ongoing plan, you will not get very far and may not be very successful

However, if you think about it carefully probably one of the number one reasons for beginning the business is eventually harvesting the profit or growth from the business and "retirement" whatever that may mean to you.

MY VIEW: *Most owners don't leave simply for the money, but they, just as simply, will not leave without it. The real challenge is to maintain the income stream you may enjoy today post-exit, after you no longer own the company. Without planning and execution, few owners can exit today and continue to maintain their lifestyle.*

Expand Your Thinking About the Future

This requires what I call "Transition Thinking". In order to plan effectively for your new future, you need to use "transition thinking" which is a dynamic way of thinking that allows it you to think more broadly and deeply about both your personal future and the future of your business. Each time you go through a life-transition you change, learn and grow. For example, take a minute right now to write down some answers to these questions:

» What life-transitions have you gone through?

» What did you learn from them?

» What "overall lessons" have you learned from your life-transitions?

» How can you apply what you've learned to this new challenge of thinking about and preparing for transitioning or exiting out of your business and moving on to a new life?

Which leads to a brief discussion of what I've discovered through my appreciation and acquisition of the CExP designation through the Business Enterprise Institute to be the "Three Universal Goals.

Universal Goal 1: *Living The Dream* – How much money do you want when you leave your business?

Universal Goal 2: *Departure Date* – When do you want to exit? How ready will you be? How long do you think it will take? How long do you think it will take your management team or children to be able to fill the roles you once filled?

Universal Goal 3: *Desired Successor* – To whom do you want to transfer the business?

CHAPTER TWO

WHAT DO I HAVE? A NEW DEFINITION OF RETIREMENT

"It's not retirement, it's the platinum years – a new state of active life."
JAMIE MOORE

When you think about retirement, the goal is to integrate your vocation, your business, and your identity by thinking of life is a journey rather than a destination.

So, the question becomes should retirement even be the goal? For me, I certainly didn't want to be working as hard as I do today when I'm 80. However, neither do I want to be of no further use to anyone else. I definitely want to have some role to play in the vast network of human cooperation and experience I think of as the "economy."

Like most people, who have attempted to play, enjoy, or master the game of handball, you may wonder why the follow-through is important because you have already hit the ball. At that point, nothing you do either well or badly during the follow-through is going to change the trajectory of the ball. The answer, paradoxically, is that if you view the moment when your hand strikes the ball as your final goal, your serve or shot will be deeply flawed. However, if you view your hand striking the ball as an "event" on your way to the final goal of a complete hit and perfect follow-through, ideally even without looking, you know you hit the ball perfectly and it will result in a "kill shot" and as all handball players agree, "happiness is a flat-rollout!"

In my view, if retirement in and of itself is your goal, your entire "shot" will be deeply flawed. You will never create or become all you could be. However, if you view your creative, business and professional life as an exciting, ongoing process with no defined expiration date, you will avoid limiting your potential.

Picture a NASCAR driver at the end of a race. Does she come to a dead stop the moment she crosses the finish line? Of course not; she only starts to slow down when she's all the way through the finish line. In fact, she doesn't see the finish line as the end of the race. So again, in my view at least, you should not see a retirement date as your finish line. You may want to consider banishing the entire idea from your mind. That's because your beliefs shape your actions far more than the facts do.

Which is also why, of course, the things that people actually believe have far more impact on their lives than the things they may nearly know as facts.

The reason that a belief in retirement as a life goal can be destructive is that it seems to form a kind of spiritual virus that can infect all of your thinking. The thought of retiring becomes a distorting lens that corrupts your view of the world around you and mislead you into missteps.

If you visualize too much that someday in your future when you will no longer "have to work" you are subconsciously slowing down already. If your goal is to reach a certain age and then retire, by the time you reach that age, your wealth and well-being will be far less than it would have been if you had reached that age with no definitive thoughts of retirement in mind.

Life Stories of "Platinum Years" Productive Longevity[1]

Myrtle Thomas. Started teaching back in the 1920s when the only qualification necessary for a teacher was a high school diploma. Eventually, of course, in order to teach one needed a college diploma. So, at the ripe age of 100 Myrtle Thomas was recently awarded her college diploma by the University of Nebraska.

Woodie Summers. Age 90, owns a barbershop in Sacramento, California, and walks back and forth to work four days every week. When asked about customers who have retired, what he says, "they all say I wish I'd never retired. I see them deteriorate." People know that if his barbershop

[1] The following stories help me discover, pursue, and develop my own personal philosophy. Based on three different sources. *Successful Aging* by Daniel J. Levitin and national summit conferences held by the Wealth Counsel of Estate Planning Attorneys and the UR Association, LLC. Daniel J. Levitin, *Successful Aging* (Published in 2002 by Penguin Random House, LLC.)

is open, Woodie is still around. "Were good until we die" he says.

Charles Hoffman. Is 91 and still practices as an attorney and Mobile Alabama – hoo ray! His recent clients: a man accused of drug possession, a husband divorcing the same wife for the third time, the estate of a deceased person with 50 beneficiaries. "There's no end", he says, of "human complications." While still in his 80s, one day in court, a young opposing attorney attacked Hoffman's integrity. "I told him, what you just step outside with me for a minute and we'll figure this out". The judge leaned over and told the young lawyer, "if I were you, I would apologize to Mr. Hoffman.". Part of the delight of practicing law into his 90s, Hoffman says, is still being able to intellectually "scrap". He adds, "and of course it's always nice to make a little money too."

Dr. Walter Watson. Age 90, is chief of obstetrics and gynecology as University Hospital in Augusta, Georgia. He usually makes his rounds at 6:30 AM most mornings. He played college football at the Little and Then coached football before going to Medical School. He plans to keep Doctoring until he can no longer be of service to Patients. When that day comes, he says, "Well of course I'll go back to Coaching."

Hazel Howard. Age 90, works at the McDonald's in Lynn Massachusetts. She says she loves being around people at the fast-food restaurant where she turns out 500 orders of fries with each shift. She still drives her 1986 Mustang to work four days a week from the ground floor of the house she shares with one of her 11 grandchildren. A year from now show retire, she says, then reconsiders: "I just had my driver's license renewed. It's good until I'm 95."

The Two Biggest Lies of the Retirement Myth[2]

NO. 1 Work has no value in and of itself. This lie is that all your work and creativity is focused on some "end" – rather than having value in and of itself. Allowing these "myths" into your brain encourages you to absorb the mindset that insists you work only to live. The truth is, you live in order to work.

NO. 2 People become less productive and less useful as they age. The second lie prompted by the retirement myth is that as time goes by you become weaker and less capable of being productive, creative, and making money. It is almost self-evident that if you are indeed getting closer and closer to retirement as you age, each passing day must be robbing you of just a little more of your creative, exciting, and money-making ability. This is the lie.

The truth is that unless your business is pounding on another fighter in an MMA ring, or charging up a field while clutching a football, each passing day makes you a more effective wealth creator and grants you added potential to be creative, productive and generate revenue. I say this because making money depends on relationships, and with the passage of time everyone should possess a larger and larger Rolodex. The joy of all of this is that you become a lot less self-centered, which means that you are better equipped to nurture and maintain your friendships and relationships.

[2] This section contains information from Rabbi Daniel Lapin, *Thou Shall Prosper* (New Jersey, John Wiley & Son 2010)

The other exciting news based on recent studies of the brain's neural plasticity and the premise of successful aging. Is that with each passing year you will often become tougher and more resilient, more experienced, you'll have much more wisdom, much better at rolling with the punches and designing your life into the future. So, of course, you become more valuable to yourself and those around you not less valuable.

Robert Lewis Stephenson said; "to travel hopefully is a better thing than to arrive." Continuing your business activities, your creative endeavors, and your personal development, is the very best way in my view of always traveling hopefully throughout your life. In this way you can "prosper" and better yet, you can help others also.

Point to Ponder

"Thank God every morning when you get up that you have something to do that day which must be done, whether you like it or not. Being forced to work and forced to do your best will breed in you temperance, self-control, diligence, strength of will, cheerfulness, contentment, and 100 virtues which the idol will never know."

CHARLES KINGSLEY

English Author and Clergyman

MY VIEW: *This ongoing discussion about retirement is an amazing and fascinating topic. Each of us get to choose our own path. For some,* *retirement may mean continuing to work doing exactly the same thing as long as one is physically able like the stories above. For others, retirement may actually mean playing golf most every day and doing absolutely nothing else. It really doesn't matter; the issue is only important to your transition or exit strategy because what you plan to do will determine your process to get there.*

So why bring the subject up in this manner? The point is that when designing a transition or exit strategy, you must give thought to what you are exiting to as a goal. My analogy, as a former football player, and now fan, is the "second-half". Too many people work their entire lives with "retirement" as their goal, only to find that it doesn't suit them or, worse for many, they literally die within two or three years after retiring. Some serious thought on the potential for how you will spend your retirement is crucial to your future happiness. Selling a business that has been your life's dream without giving any thought at all to the second half could be a monumental mistake.

As we will discuss more thoroughly in Part II sometimes the best transition or exit strategy is not to actually leave the business at all but rather to make yourself completely irrelevant to the business. In other words, the business itself continues operating without your day-to-day input while generating an ongoing cash flow that you continue to enjoy as the owner-creator-investor.

CHAPTER THREE

WHAT ARE THE ROADBLOCKS?

EXAMPLE 1

Systems and Roles in Place

"As a new venture develops and grows, the roles and relationships of the original entrepreneurs inexorably change. If the founders refused to accept this, they will stunt the business and may even destroy it. But even among the founders who can accept that they themselves need to do something, if you know how to tackle changing their own roles and relationships."
PETER DRUCKER

What do you want from your transition or exit strategy when you retire? Do you want to sell your business? Do you want to put your business on auto-pilot? Do you want to "cash out and move on"* and

* *Cash Out Move On* by John H. Brown with Kevin M. Short.

perhaps put your money into another venture? Any of these results are possible. The idea is that you need to plan for the result and then implement the plan that has been designed. Creating this written business owners roadmap isn't necessarily going to be easy but the end result will definitely be exciting and worth the effort.

For example, some time ago we help the business owner restructure his business and put together a five-year plan initially to sell to a third-party buyer. However, when we completed the plan, he changed his mind looked at his friends and families and said "what part of $1 million a year in income and working less than 20 hours a week for only 20 weeks a year don't you understand?" So, in an interesting way our client was "retired". He was the investor in his business and enjoyed the cash flow generator without having to spend 60 to 70 hours a week working in his business. In contrast, he worked 15 to 20 hours per week "on" his business the systems that he had put in place in his business provided the means by which the clients were engaged, served, serviced, and retained as a foundation for repeat business.

EXAMPLE 2

Other Reasons to Have a Roadmap[3]

Sometimes a transition or exit are forced upon a business by outside events: the death of an owner or employee, the bankruptcy of a large supplier or customer, changes in the economy, a worldwide pandemic.

[3] This section contains information from John H. Brown, *Exit Planning The Definitive Guide* (Business Enterprise Press 2016)

John Brown, the founder of the Business Enterprise Institute shares this story. "Many years ago, I created an estate plan For Ralph Cabrini, the owner of a thriving general construction company. Ralph was married and had two young children. He had a couple of key employees who managed all of the company's projects. As part of our estate planning discussion, I suggested to Ralph that he consider doing something (from the life time planning standpoint) to ensure that his two key people would stay with the company for the long haul. Ralph, with a wave of his hand and a smirk, dismissed my concern, saying "I don't worry at all about them leaving, I pay them plenty." Two months after the completion of his estate plan Ralph died. "Fortunately," I thought, "at least his estate is in good shape." But I was wrong. Three months after his death the business, and Ralph's estate were bankrupt.

What happened to Ralph's family and business was a painful lesson for me, and hopefully an instructive one for you. Shortly after Ralph's death, his two key employees realized that the business was not going to survive without him. While they felt badly for Ralph's family, they decided that their first responsibility was to support their own families. They found jobs with new employers who had contacted them shortly after Ralph's death. Without their supervision, the projects the company had underway came to an abrupt halt. Lack of progress put the construction contracts into default, and the bond company eventually foreclosed on the company's assets. The bond company then threatened to file suit against Ralph's estate for the bond default.

In only 90 days the business and the value of Ralph's estate had evaporated. The one saving grace was the revocable life insurance trust we had put in place for the benefit of Ralph's family. We had funded it with a significant amount of life insurance, but not nearly enough to replace the income stream both Ralph and Ralph's business produced every year.

For years I thought about how we could have prevented the carnage to Ralph's business and family. How could we have made sure, that in the event of Ralph's death, his company would compete and complete its projects in the business (even if unable to continue in the long term) could be liquidated in a financially responsible manner? Even more optimistically, what could've been done to ensure the business could continue if Ralph didn't?"

The point is that both business continuity and estate planning are vital components of the transition or exit planning process. More often than not, the reverse is not true. In my experience, many estate planning advisors do not differentiate between an owner's business – which (without proper planning) depends primarily upon the owner showing up every day – and his or her other assets (e.g. an investment portfolio), which ordinarily do not.

The bottom line is that every owner of any age should pay attention to all of the elements of transition or exit planning, even if they don't call it or think of it as "exit planning". Value drivers and business continuity are just for "mature" owners doesn't every owner want to grow and preserve business value and to know that his or her family's financial security is not dependent upon his or her long life and good health?

Ralph's estate planning attorney is to be commended for his suggestion. Unfortunately, however, when Ralph summarily dismissed the idea, I believe that the attorney should have pushed Ralph for an answer and to take action.

You don't need to over pay to work with advisers who will push back when you are about to make a poor decision. What you can afford is to work with advisers who will not push back we will never know whether a proactive stance would have changed Ralph's mind. We do know, however, that the incremental legal fee, if any, for such proactivity would have paled in comparison to the price Ralph's family ultimately paid.

MY VIEW: *Based upon my many years of experience, I've come to realize that most estate planning advisors seldom asked the necessary questions of business owners to determine what actually needs to be done to ensure that an owner's lifetime business and personal goals are attained if the owner does not make it to the planned departure date as a result of death or permanent disability. Isn't the whole idea to make sure your business continues even if you don't?*

To avoid such a result there are four critical questions to ask. If I die or become permanently disabled tomorrow:

» Will my family be able to maintain the lifestyle I want for them?

» Will my business survive?

» Will my business transfer according to my wishes?

Will my other goals, including my values-based goals, be achieved?

All of these questions could be examined, addressed, and answered by a well-planned written transition or exit plan strategy. To know where you want to end up on a trip, a good map is an indispensable tool. In business, your transition or exit strategy is like a roadmap. The idea is you plan out where it is you want to be and what your goals are, create a written roadmap, and then execute the plan.

The same thinking and strategy applies to a business that has co-owners. Obviously in the beginning everybody's happy and friendly. However, if something goes wrong, regardless of the cause, this happy friendship can dissipate very quickly. Having a transition or exit planning strategy in place at the beginning of the business through proper planning and a well thought out and well drafted Buy/Sell Agreement (see Appendix C) provides the defined path to the exit, even in the unlikely event that the co-owners are not even speaking to each other or cannot agree on anything. The point is, the transition or exit strategy gives them a tool to just exit, saving the need to fight about how to exit.

Continuing along this line of thinking, your transition or exit strategy is also an escape hatch that can limit your liability upon and after your exit. For example, you may want to protect your employees after your exit.

That being said, more often than not the most important consideration is that if you do not have a written plan for your transition or exit strategy you can almost guarantee that you will not exit "in style" which has previously discussed means maximum money for you, minimum taxes to Darth Vader (the IRS) and the elimination of any hassles or messes.

CHAPTER FOUR

USING A TRANSITION OR EXIT STRATEGY TO CREATE AND PROTECT WEALTH

"There are many truths of which the full meaning cannot be realized until personal experience has brought it home."
JOHN STUART MILL

So far, we have been talking about transition or exit strategies as they relate to leaving a business or career. As discussed previously, this idea and thinking comes from what we've all been taught by our parents and in our schools that the key to happiness and success is to get a good education, and a good job, save their money until they have enough to live without the job. This leads to perhaps the wrong conclusion that the only reason we work is to be able to pay our bills and eventually when we have enough money to pay her bills without working voilà retirement!

I want to take a different view. I want to address something that was never taught in school. In fact, we may have been criticized for being lazy or not ambitious had the subject come up. The reality is; however, it would've been very beneficial for us to understand the concept of wealth accumulation and protection. Query, in all of your schooling or other life experience have you ever had a class that covered the idea of wealth accumulation and protection? Think about it, 12 years of school through high school, then some of us go to college, then graduate school. Personally, I went to school for three years beyond college with law school and since then have taken many advanced estate planning, exit planning, and taxation courses. Never once do I remember anyone bringing up the topic of creating, accumulating, and protecting wealth through business ownership.

So, as we begin, may I ask you something? Why are you interested in creating wealth? The first step to creating wealth is to avoid buying into the myth that is harder to create wealth today than it was before not true, there are more millionaires per capita now than at any other time in history.

If you talk to people who have achieved success even on a multimillion-dollar level, the issue is not lack of opportunity, but rather a bombardment of more opportunities than any one person can effectively deal with. Part of creating wealth is developing the ability to recognize opportunities. Once you do, they are virtually everywhere.

This leads us to the next step regarding your instincts. That is, developing the power of discernment. That is the exciting challenge today in terms of creating, accumulating, and protecting personal wealth which is to develop a power of discernment, and ability to recognize your own strengths and weaknesses, and to go forward regarding any opportunity that suits you.

Dr. Stephen R. Covey, the author of *The Seven Habits of Highly Effective People*, explained it well when he said the leader is one who climbs the tallest tree, surveys the entire situation, and yells, "wrong jungle!" On the other hand, look to the busy, distracted, so-called efficient managers and workers say? "Shut up, we may be in the wrong jungle but we're making progress." I would not only echo Dr. Covey's words, but I would add this thought, echoed by many authors recently Jim Collins in his recent book Great By Choice, good can actually be the enemy of great.

One of the crucial concepts that we have already devoted a lot of coverage to and will continue to do so in the rest of this book is simply this. If you start or buy a business, make sure you have a mindset that includes selling it. Those who fail to include a "transition or exit strategy" and their plans are in danger of becoming slaves to their career job or business.

The idea of making your business an investment instead of a job will be discussed in Part II, and is the key to the creation, accumulation, and preservation of wealth through business ownership.

That being said, however, please consider and hopefully enjoy the next section first.

Live Too Long or Die Too Soon

The Longer Your Live, The Longer You Live.
But Once You're Dead, You're Dead

Let's get right to the point. What is your money really doing for you? Did you ever say to yourself, "someday when I have more money, I'll..."? Have you actually done all of the things you always wanted to do? Are you doing what you want to do now? Are you spending your time, talents and resources doing what you really want to do? What are your goals? If you could have the perfect situation, what would it be?

These are the questions I ask all my clients in order to achieve clarity about their vision for life, business and finances. Getting a concise, articulate list of goals usually requires a lot more probing on my part, however. Most often the answers to these questions are tangled in an individual's perception of how things currently are. When setting goals, people are often influenced by other people's opinions, or limited by what they think they already know about money, taxes, etc. For example, many people tell me they would love to sell a problematic building or stock. But then they say, "the capital gains taxes are just so high I can't sell it." They don't know there are several tricks that could implement to eliminate the capital gains tax on the sale of such assets. A lack a person's knowledge or a misconception of technical issues often limits that person's options. Such self-limitation must be overcome if optimum results are to be achieved.

We are all trapped by our limited knowledge. It is this limitation which ultimately interferes with our ability to achieve wide-angle macro vision, to dream, set goals or move ahead. When clients say they cannot sell an appreciated asset without paying capital gains taxes, I could immediately jump into a teacher mode and explain various techniques for avoiding the payment of capital gains taxes. However, it is more helpful to stay focused on defining the vision and then explain the various techniques or tactics after all the goals are identified. Took me a while to figure this out. Crystal-clear vision and goal definition are so important that they must come first.

If we cannot articulate and stand by our vision and goals, we become moving targets. No one can help us; we cannot help ourselves if we keep changing our mind or redefining our goals. It's crucial that we devote the necessary time to establish goals which are true to our wide-angle vision and to what we ultimately desire so that we can stick to them. When developing goals, remember that you can still build in enough flexibility to allow for changes and to your own evolution.

So just how can we work together to overcome the many obstacles that would interfere with our vision and goal-setting process? It's really rather simple; can be summed up with this question: "if you could wave a magic wand and completely ignore the tax and investment laws, or your perception of them, what would your perfect situation be?" We need to free ourselves of our misconceptions and ignore what we think we know, and concentrate on what we really want.

We also need to make sure that we are actually setting goals and not just focusing on strategies. Using football as a metaphor, the football team enters the field; their goal is to win the game. However, there may be several strategies they can employ to achieve that goal depending on the strengths and weaknesses of the team, their opponent, and the circumstances. The goal or objective is the desired end result: to win. The strategy and tactics are the means used to achieve the goal. The same is true in the transition or exit planning game.

Strategies available to help keep your wealth will be fulfilled through a variety of tactics. However, when setting financial lifestyle goals, many people forget to concentrate on the goals and spend too much time concentrating on the strategies, or worst, the tools. It's literally the difference between clarity and certainty. You can be very clear about your goals, like the football team, about the play to run and everyone's role or job within the play. However, you can't be certain about the outcome – a touchdown. The point is, more clarity tends to lead us to more certainty. As you might imagine, we have encountered many different personalities, perceptions, and paradigms.

We have seen our clients utilize a variety of methods and mechanisms to build their estates and accumulate wealth. We have come to understand that it takes a certain focus in mindset to accumulate wealth and build an estate. However, it requires a much different focus and approach to plan, protect, preserve, and make the most of your wealth once you've earned it. You can be extremely effective at earning money investing your net worth only to find yourself empty-handed because you failed to manage your wealth and avoid various pitfalls.

What pitfalls am I talking about? Changing economic or market conditions, capital gains taxes, income and excise taxes, estate taxes, litigation, changing state and federal laws, in accurate or incompetent advice, failure to act upon good advice, and many other financial pitfalls can rob you of your wealth. How many times have you seen celebrities or professional athletes in the news who have lost significant fortunes because they have put their trust in dishonest or incompetent people or failed to manage or truly diversify their wealth effectively?

One of the wealth advisors I work with likes to use the metaphor of a hot air balloon. As the balloon fills with air, the yellow, red and blue silks expand. The balloon begins to rise above the ground, heading for beautiful skies. Just as the balloon is about to escape gravities hold, it is yanked to a stop. Tethered to the ground by ropes, the balloon is unable to free itself.

That hot air balloon is you and everyone who wants to make the most of their wealth. Your wealth is the hot air which should enable you to rise and reach your goals; however, there are ropes attached that may prevent you from reaching your true goal – freedom. These ropes are different for everyone. See if any of these common restraints are pulling on you and holding you down:

» Conflicting advice or information from different sources.

» Too much or too little information.

» When you wait for the tax laws to change.

» Rental or investment property headaches.

» Decline in real estate or other asset value.

- Interest rate fluctuations.
- Rising costs.
- Heirs or other family members worried that you might jeopardize their inheritance.
- Conflicting retirement options and indecision.
- Procrastination about making necessary changes.
- Fear of making any changes at all.
- And the list goes on...

Then There is That Huge Rope Attached to Your Balloon Called Congress[4]

I'm sure it comes as no surprise at all that the "boys and girls along the Potomac" want a huge piece of your life in your estate now while you're alive and again after you die. Income taxes, capital gains taxes, excise and estate taxes and many other tax issues are pulling on you. Some of them may be holding you down, preventing you from reaching new heights and going where you want to go.

There's an old tale from India about a wise Raja who wanted to study an important aspect of human nature. The Raja gathered six blind

[4] This section contains information from Bruce Raymond Wright, *The Wright Exit Strategy* (The Wright Company 1997) "But My Business Is Different" Value Drivers.

gurus together and asked them to define a creature by touch. Because all the gurus were blind since birth, they had never seen such a creature. To make certain the gurus would not be prejudiced by previous descriptions they may have heard, they were not told what kind of animal it was.

Each blind guru was assigned to a different part of the creature and allowed to touch only that portion of the animal to which he was assigned. The first guru touch the tusk and said, "this animal is like a spear". Second the roof felt the trunk and declared, "this animal is like a snake.". Feeling the ear, the third guru exclaimed, "this animal is like a fan." Fourth guru touch the creature's front leg and announced, "this animal is like a tree." The fifth guru after patting the creature's side declared, "this animal is like a wall." Finally, the six gurus grasped the tail and proclaimed, "this animal is like a rope."

The six blind gurus began arguing over who was right and who was wrong. Because each of these gurus had an ego and pride, as most of us do, the argument became quite heated. At this point, the wise Raja who had set up the contest stepped in and said, "the elephant is a large animal, made up of different parts. Each of you has a knowledge of only one part. To find out the whole truth, you must gain knowledge of all the parts and put them together. In order to do this, you must set aside your ego and pride and realize you may not have all the knowledge necessary to comprehend the whole elephant." This story exemplifies the essence of macro or big picture thinking.

In some ways, we can all be like blind gurus. Trying to get an accurate perspective or find the truth in life, finances, etc. Which can be very difficult, especially if you are too close to the situation. The most accurate and helpful knowledge is often gained when we step back from the situation and try to look at it from different angles. In order to do this effectively, we often need to have help from several sources and for several reasons. First, if it is about us or our personal situation, the closer we are to an issue, the more emotionally we tend to be. The more emotional we become, the less subjective we are. Secondly, we cannot be experts in everything important to our success. We don't know all the angles where they are or even everything we should look for. Thus, we often need third-party help to accurately perceive and overcome obstacles or take advantage of opportunities.

When we are introduced to new clients, the conversation usually begins with a very particular problem to solve. People tend to focus on one specific issue, not the whole picture. They want to know how to fix that problem now, yet really is it in someone's best interest to proceed with any solutions at this point in time. Many people don't realize that every action they take concerning their assets may very well impact their entire net worth.

Therefore, it is critical that we have a clear understanding of the whole "elephant," the complete financial and personal long-term vision and goals, before we undertake any critical changes. It's even safer to say, before we undertake any changes, most people do not know enough about financial issues, tax issues, etc., To differentiate what is critical and what is not, and what all of the ramifications might be.

For example, as it relates to estate planning, the most common definition that we have heard around the country is, "when you're dead, how are we going to divide up your stuff?" That's **Level I** estate planning.

Level II is, "how do you generate maximum living benefits from your estate during your lifetime, and then how do you most effectively distribute your estate to your heirs, family, or charitable causes after you pass away?" This is a much better approach than **Level I**, but there is a higher level, **Level III**.

Level III is where true big picture legacy and wealth accumulation and protection planning actually takes place.

Level III asks, "What is your 100-year plan? What are you going to do while you are alive to fulfill your 100-year plan, and how will your vision and goals be carried out after you're gone?"

This holistic approach requires much more than just taking care of yourself now and distributing money later to your heirs. With a 100-year plan, you are creating a legacy while you are alive and furthering that legacy after you are gone. If you are over 60 years of age, you may think that a 100-your plan doesn't make any sense for you, but it really does. If you and your heirs can adopt and live this 100-year philosophy of life, how much more effective will you be than those who live in a day-to-day, moment-to-moment, rudimentary existence? We had one client who is in his late 70s say to us, "I don't even buy green bananas anymore, because that's how long-term my thinking is. How on earth can I get motivated to set up a 100-year plan?" Establishing a 100-year plan is not an easy task, but then almost nothing of worthwhile value is perceived as easy.

An important observation: Even the greatest teachers cannot teach an unwilling student.

Most effective advisors know they can only help clients who are willing to replace ambiguity with crystal-clear vision. Being clear about your vision and what your best interests are gives advisors the clarity they need to protect, serve, and further your best interests. Committed to writing and broken down into manageable goals, strategies, tactics, tools, time-lines and benchmarks, you will have a written roadmap. Such a roadmap not only provides clarity of purpose and how you will achieve what you want, it also assigns accountability and responsibility to succeed.

PART II

CHANGING YOUR ROLE AND CHANGING THE BUSINESS

CHAPTER FIVE

HOW TO CREATE A BUSINESS THAT A BUYER CAN'T RESIST BUYING BY MAKING YOURSELF IRRELEVANT

"We have met the enemy... And they is us."
POGO, WALT KELLY

FOLLOW THE YELLOW BRICK ROAD. There may be "50 Ways to Leave Your Lover" but there are only four things you can do with your business. Before beginning the process of designing a transition or exit strategy, it's very important to define your roles and your starting point. What kind of business do you have now? There are basically four types of business or roles you can assume in your business.

PLAYER. What do players do? Well, of course they "play". Are you the main driving force, producer or technician in your business? If so, like many businesses it's not a business is all it's just really a job. As the owner you're really just trading your hours for dollars. The only buyer for a business that is really just like a job, is another person who wants that job.

COACH. What do coaches do? Well, of course they "coach" the players. Like a coach your business may very well be your passion. You been there from the beginning with the birthing and you've watched it grow and may find it difficult to let it go. Because the owner conceives, nurtures, and develops the team it's easy to fall in love with team. This sometimes leads to the fact that an owner waits way too long about selling.

Doesn't matter whether it's a good team or a bad team. It's the owner's team. The next thing this sometimes happens as the owner cannot let go of the team. The owner also usually has too high of an opinion of the business and its actual sale price or value. Psychologically, the turnover of the business to another owner becomes an obstacle. Even subconsciously, owners are sometimes able to make progress in beginning or consummating the sale.

PLAYER/COACH. Because you have to fill both roles and can't let go sometimes what started out as a business becomes a nightmare. Which you up at night keeps you constantly worrying about everything. Is the team going to win lose or draw? I wonder what the competition is doing? What about the league itself? Sometimes the business can turn into a money pit.

For example, a business that has no real solid customer base. A business that loses one of its major players/employees for any reason dislike a major injury to a key player in a team. Such a business is probably not very stable or sellable.

OWNER. What do owners do? Well, not unlike the owner of an NFL football team or other professional sports team, by analogy, owners only have to do two things. One, make sure that the product or service that the business offers is exactly what the customers need. Two, measure the actual return on investment of the business as an investment. All of this of course is dependent upon the systems that have been installed and the quality of the team managing those systems. For example, as an owner could you take a month off and have no contact at all with your business without it affecting it. That way the owner is similar to an investor in the stock market. His money is at work not the owner. And isn't it interesting that in a sense, the more irrelevant the owner is to the business the more valuable it is.

I encourage you to step back and take a look at your business. If you fit into any of the first three categories, now is not the time to delay or procrastinate. Rather, begin to take action now to plan your transition or exit strategy so that your business can operate without you. One of the concepts we have learned from our affiliation with the Business Enterprise Institute, in this area has to do with helping the business owner envision a change in their role from "hands-on and head down to hands off and head up."

This does not have to be scary. In fact, the changes could very well be exciting. The first change requires you to focus your efforts on growing the business – beyond your capabilities – if it is to have sufficient value to fund your post – exit financial independence.

Secondly, you must change your role in the company from being the hub to being just a spoke. Owners who are spokes retain an important role in their companies but their companies can function and grow well without them.

Third, as you make the first two changes, you can gain the freedom (and time!) That comes from fewer duties and responsibilities. With more time, you have the opportunity (and I would argue, the task) to explore and develop non—business pursuits. Business growth will be stunted if the owners fail to change, and the company itself will fail to evolve.

This is true not only in business but in life. To quote Charles Darwin, "it is not the strongest of the species that survives, or the most intelligent, but the one most responsive to change."

As you think about and make these changes ideally you will come to an inflection point which is when owners must decide whether to run the business based on personal objectives or to create an organization that doesn't require the hands – on involvement of its owner.

An example would be to business owners who started their business at the same time, but whom ended up in a very different place. The difference between the business that cannot be sold in the business that can be successfully transitioned well achieving the owner's goals and aspirations and even a business that could become an industry player, results from the actions owners take to change their role and relationship to their business.

Lastly, as you think about your role ask yourself this question quote "where can the company best use my talents, strengths, abilities and experience?" We believe it is an owner's decision to transform his or her relationship to the company as the company approaches critical inflection points that separates a business that cannot be sold, from an industry player or one that attracts the attention of buyers.

POP QUIZ
Is Your Business An Investment or a Job?

At the expense of being somewhat redundant, let's revisit this important issue one more time. Here are some questions. If you were called to jury duty and selected to serve on a jury for several weeks, what would happen to your business?

What if you had a car accident on the way home from work next week and you couldn't go to work in your business for the next two or three months what would happen to your business?

Can you take a day off, week off, or month off and leave the office behind parents no phone calls, emails, or calling into the office)'s and still not affect your income at all?

Well, once again then depending on your answers to these questions you may not have a business investment you have a job. Maybe a great job in a well-paid job but it's still a job. Business investors, key employees, and even family members don't buy jobs they buy cash flow and profit.

MY VIEW: *When business owners begin to think about transitioning or exiting from their business, they need to consider the facts and their view of their business as either a job or as an investment. This distinction is critical in facilitating any kind of transition or exit because when the transaction is complete, the owners will be left with a financial reward. This reward can be structured in many different ways. There may be a lump – sum amount of cash for 100% of the value of the business delivered to the owner at the closing of the sale transaction. Often, however, a large portion of the value will be received at a date after the closing transaction.*

For example, if a business is transferring to key employees, or to family members, there may be no lump sum at all that the closing but merely a stream of income transferring to the business owner over time.

So, the idea is as a business owner to picture this sum of money in your mind, then you can see that your business is truly an investment. Instead, most owners see their business as a job. Often, they see themselves as the boss, king or queen of the castle, so to speak. It is dangerous for business owners to be complacent about having a job, particularly when it comes to transition or exit strategy planning. When business owners begin to view their businesses as investments and not jobs, they begin making better long-term financial decisions.

Value Drivers That Make the Business An Investment

Your decisions regarding what to do next with your business will be crucial in determining whether you will have a business that will sell for the best price possible or may make the business impossible to sell. If you pay attention to what we call "value drivers" in your business you will be able to create a peace of mind and security that a well-planned, effective transition or exit strategy can provide.

Without a basic understanding of these value drivers, it is extremely hard to plan a transition or exit strategy. Because most businesses involve lots of hard work and sacrifice, that fact alone can sometimes cloud the perception of the actual value internal operation of the business. By examining, and implementing appropriately these value drivers the value can dramatically increase. Procrastinating or ignoring examining these strategies will also hurt the potential value. Secondly, failing to have a written roadmap for the transition or exit, by whatever routes, means that planning the transition or exit will most likely fail.

As often quoted by many authors, most people do not plan to fail, they fail to plan.

Back again to the Cheshire cat and Yogi Berra, if you don't know where you want to go it doesn't matter what route you take. Without examining, and implementing these value drivers will lead back to the idea of your just having a job and not an investment.

Your written roadmap must take into consideration something many people call "WIIFM", or "what's in it for me?" From the perspective buyer's viewpoint. In other words what exactly will the buyer be looking for in the business? Having a good handle on and implementing and improving the value drivers in your business will help you be much better prepared on the backend.

"But My Business is Different" Value Drivers[5]

This is something we hear from business owners all the time. The answer though is almost irrelevant. The idea is how do we accelerate the growth and value of our business? The most significant factor that it impacts your ability to leave your company – successfully or unsuccessfully – is creating a company with transferable value which leads to our brief discussion of value drivers.

[5] This section contains information from John H. Brown, *Exit Planning The Definitive Guide* (Business Enterprise Press 2016)

Transferable value is what your business is worth, to someone else, without you. The company was strong value drivers can demand (and receive) a higher multiple on the same amount of EBITDA (earnings before interest, taxes, depreciation, and appreciation) that can accompany with average value drivers.

The primary value drivers are:

1. Next - level management
2. Operating systems demonstrated to increase sustainability of cash flow
3. Diversified customer base
4. Proven growth strategy
5. Recurring revenue that is sustainable and resistant to "commoditize nation"
6. Good and improving cash flow
7. Demonstrated scalability
8. Competitive advantage
9. Financial foresight and controls.

Unfortunately, we do not have the time or space in this book to completely unpack all of these for you. What follows is a very brief description of each one.

However, if you'd like to learn more about this topic, we teach a workshop specifically on the topic of Value Drivers. All you have to do is reach out to us and inquire about that and will be happy to talk with you about it.

Next – Level Management. Next – level management is the mother of all value drivers. It is not only the most critical value driver, but it must be management that oversees, manages, the growth of all the other value drivers. It supports and strengthens all the other value drivers.

Operating Systems Improve Sustainability Of Cash Flows. The establishment and documentation of standard business procedures and systems demonstrate to buyers that a business can maintain profitability after the sale and after you have left. The establishment and use of systems contribute to cash flow creation and increase its sustainability.

Diversified Customer Base. Buyers typically look for a custom base in which no single client accounts for more than 10% of total sales. A diversified customer base insulates your company from the loss of a major customer. For example, if your top three customers generate 40% of your sales, a buyer would be concerned if one or more of them left upon learning that you sold your company.

Proven Growth Strategy. Even if you expect to retire tomorrow, it makes sense to have a written plan describing future growth and how you will achieve that growth in the context of industry dynamics and demands for your company's products.

Recurring Revenue Is Sustainable And Resistant to "Commoditization". You may wish to view this as to two value drivers. One, recurring, sustainable revenue and, two, having products or services resistant to commoditization.

Good And Improving Cash Flow. Ultimately, all value drivers contribute to stable and predictable cash flow. Today you can start increasing your company's cash flow by simply focusing on ways to operate your business more efficiently, increasing product to the tea, and decreasing costs.

This alone may not create sufficient growth to allow you to achieve your objectives on time. This value driver depends on the efficient operation of the other value drivers.

Demonstrated Scalability. Can your company improve its profit margins if it increased its revenue? Think about designing a computer app like Angry Birds. There is a fixed cost to design and test, but additional sales do not increase those costs. Yes, scalability is a bit more difficult if you own a hardware store but not impossible if your hardware store enjoys high profitability and strong revenue growth.

Competitive Advantage. To paraphrase Michael Porter of Harvard University's Business School, competitive advantage is the product or service that a company offers – either better or more cheaply – over time than does its competitors. Your company's competitive advantage is the reason your customers buy from you instead of from your competitors.

Financial Foresight And Controls. Like recurring revenue, this value driver has two aspects. The first relates to financial controls or reporting. Many companies lack reliable financial reporting to such an extent that buyers can determine what the company has or track the source of his revenues. Usually, this problem is correctable, but it takes time to do so the second aspect is less apparent, but more important. If your company is to grow substantially and quickly, it "has to be fed". As you create a growth plan for your business, you must project the cash flow costs of implementing it.

In conclusion, growing and creating transferable value requires a reassessment of your role in the business as previously discussed, as well as creating value drivers that enhance the "transferable" aspect of business value. Growing transferable value to the level needed to attain your goals likely requires skills and experience beyond your pay grade. Most owners, including me, need to look to others – next level management and outside consultants – who have the requisite experience and skill.

The bottom line is when you strip away the specifics of a single business or industry, the basic value drivers of all businesses are exactly the same. Sometimes you can learn more about what you can do to improve your business by studying how another industry is successful than by studying the competitors in your own business.

CHAPTER SIX

SYSTEMS & STRUCTURES THAT WILL TRANSFORM YOUR BUSINESS INTO AN ASSET[6]

Let's take a look briefly at the fundamental structure for any business. The idea being to transform your business into one that buyers will drool over. Remember, the most valuable and salable businesses are those that are in fact a true investment for a potential buyer instead of just an employment opportunity. In order for the business to function as an investment, implement and take advantage of the above value drivers, and thrive, it's crucial that the business should take advantage of the following six systems.

[6] This chapter is based on information and training received from the systems and processes created by Ben Glass, Founder and CEO; Great Legal Marketing and Ben Glass Law, www.greatlegalmarketing.com

EXAMPLE ONE

Client Attraction

How do you get your clients or customers? In many of his books, which I highly recommend, author Dan Kennedy and marketing guru talks about the ways you can increase the income from your business.

As he puts it, there are only three ways to increase business income. One get new customers. Two get your existing customers to buy more frequently, and three increase the amount the customers are spending with you most expensive way may be getting new customers. It is sometimes more efficient and cheaper to increase the amount your existing customers or clients buy or use. The fascinating question that is the subject of another example that will be discussed is: do you have a robust system to capture information for your customers and clients in order to retain them and leverage them to do no more business.

Your client attraction system is like creating a funnel that inputs a constant stream of potential new avatar customers or clients. You put leads, direct, virtual, Internet, direct mail, pay per click ads, etc. into the top of your funnel in those potential clients pre—sell themselves, eventually coming out of the end of the funnel ready to become a new customer or client.

EXAMPLE TWO

Client Engagement System

regardless of how many perspective clients or customers flow into or out of your funnel the thing that really matters is how many of them actually become clients? Just like your favorite fishing hole, there can be hundreds of fish swimming by your lure any given time. The fish don't like the bait or using, they're not going to bite and you have peanut butter and jelly for dinner instead.

The idea is that since what you offer to clients or customers will be of benefit to them you have an obligation to help them say yes. So, are they saying yes or are they merely checking you out and not moving ahead? Are they confused by the material and offers and information that you're presenting? Have you tested your materials, reports, and offers to see what in fact is the most effective with a potential customer? Again, back to Dan Kennedy, the marketing guru who recommends that your client engagement system be standardized, reviewed, and tested as much as possible

How do you recreate the ideal experience each time? This involves planning, organizing, and scripting exactly what happens when someone calls for an appointment or request some information. You then send them an introductory meeting package or other information or reports that pre-sells the client or the customer. You then meet with the prospect in a pleasing, well-organized environment that is conducive to doing business together. Lastly, when you do meet with the prospect you have an organized process, checklist, and scripting to make sure you are covering all of the materials in the same way each and every time. In that regard we highly recommend the book by Claire Enns "The Win Without Pitching Manifesto".

It does not matter what business you are in; the same principles and systemization of your process applies.

EXAMPLE THREE

Client Service System

Fantastic, you captured the client, now what? You've heard it said over and over and over again it's all about service! Everything before the client engagement began is terrific, but unless you get the work done and get it done well, on time, under promised and over delivered, nothing else is important.

So, what is your process at this point? Is it literally planned out step-by-step or will you just wing it? McDonald's of course is the classic example. What about your business? Once the "order is placed", what happens next? Do you reinvent the wheel every time? Or do you have specific procedures in a process to follow every time? Every one of your clients and customers deserves to have the same experience and receive the same outstanding process every time. The new client or customer experience should be choreographed from the moment of beginning to the final delivery of the completed product or service.

Similarly, as a relates to any follow-up or ongoing maintenance system that you may have.

The goal of this type of process, planning, and consistency creates what one author calls "raving fans". These customers or clients then recommend your business to their friends, family, and colleagues. The idea here is that your client attraction system does not have to work nearly as hard to keep the funnel full.

More importantly, when the entire process and experiences systemized, your present becomes less essential because you made it possible to have your team create and provide the same experience that you would have given. When that happens, you are taking the steps to make yourself more irrelevant and thus make your business more valuable.

Does Your Business Have a Purple Cow? Are You Wearing a Red Shirt?

Seth Godin wrote a book called The Purple Cow about the things that set businesses apart and makes them noticeable. The picture he describes is this:

You are driving down the road, and you look over at a bunch of cows in the field. Brown cows, black cows, spotted cows and a purple cow. Wait a minute! A purple cow! Wow you gotta be kidding? I can't believe my eyes! Did you see that purple cow in that field over there? I've got to call my friends; they're never going to believe this!

So, the obvious question is are you the purple cow in the field of Brown cows? What is it about your business that sets it apart from others? Why would anyone want to do business with you as opposed to your competition?

The second idea supposedly comes from a story about Henry Ford. The story goes that Mr. Ford while walking around the manufacturing facility of this company was approached by a worker who asked him this question. "Mr. Ford, can you tell me what it is I can do to excel here at your company and move up the ladder from where I am now?" Mr. Ford replied, "Well, look around you do see everyone here not working very and wearing a blue shirt?" "Yes" replied the worker. "Well," replied Mr. Ford, "The answer is pretty obvious. All you have to do is wear a red shirt and work like hell!"

So, the next obvious question is when people look at you, and your business, and your workers and associates and teammates, who is it that's wearing a red shirt and working like hell? And what if anything can you do to enhance or create a culture where you have more hard-working "red shirts."

EXAMPLE FOUR
Team Training and Accountability

At the risk of being redundant once again we have to bring up McDonald's. Isn't it true that it doesn't matter whether you're in Los Angeles, or Chicago, you always get the exact same hamburger? As we discussed before a lot of this depends on systemization. However, the second important principle is "training and accountability".

Let's use our law firm as an example. We are part of a very extensive and robust training and implementation program called Great Legal Marketing. One of the key principles we've been taught for our marketing is that it's all designed for the most part to get people to call our law firm. The phone rings. Who is going to talk to that potential client? What exactly are they going to say? How will we know what is said? Do we have a script that has been taught to this person? Do we have someone randomly call our law firm every now and then just to see what the person answering the phone is actually saying? Is there someone on this person's team to which they are accountable who listens periodically to make sure what is being said in why?

Again, looking out our law firm, do we have specific revenue benchmarks that our team has to meet? Is our team financially compensated when they meet or exceed these benchmarks? What about other incentive? What about monthly, quarterly and annual team and leadership planning meetings.

The point is that you will discover just as we have that you will have a strong, productive, and motivated team when they are trained, accountable, responsible, and responsive. Systems and benchmarks don't invent themselves. If you're waiting for your team to develop the systems and processes don't hold your breath. It just will not happen. You, as the owner must take charge.

MY VIEW: *Your team needs to have a written job description, or rather performance contracts, not a long-written thesis, but rather spreadsheets for example or other graphic ways to detail the specific tasks and performance benchmarks required of them. The best way to do this is to make sure that the benchmarks are specific, understandable, measurable, attainable, and consistent its. Lastly, there must be some type of uplifting, honest, and team focused feedback system including performance incentives.*

EXAMPLE FIVE

What Are Your Numbers

One of the most interesting and fascinating things I discovered when we first began to start and develop the law firm was this thought I'll share with you that just because someone is a good professional, advisor, or technician, does not mean they are qualified to own their own business. I discovered the skill sets are not the same, and in fact, good business owner skills required that you not be the, technician, professional, or advisor all the time. Remember, again, as previously mentioned by Dr. Covey and Jim Collins, if you are always working in your business, you do not have the time to work on your business.

Consequently, how do you know when you are doing well? Some business owners are comfortable just to know they have some money in the bank. However, sometimes the money in the bank was because we are not paying the bills. For example, what tools, and metrics, and programs do you use to measure the internal return on investment of your own business?

As a former athlete, and current sports fan, I loved it that there were always measurements to gauge performance. In business, there are measurements to gauge your success as well. Let's keep in mind that the goal of any business is to make money for the owner. That goal may be secondarily to pursue the owner's lover passion, but the business is there for one main reason: to make money for the owner.

However, your goal as a savvy business owner should be even higher: to make a lot of money. As a business owner, you assume the risk of the liability for everything, employees, rent, expenses etc. You could have a regular job or career instead without nearly as much risk. But your goal is to create a business that generates a cash flow stream. However, it can't just be enough cash flow to keep the boat afloat.

We find that a business can also be evaluated on what we call a "discretionary cash flow" basis that does not require the owner to participate which can make the business worth many times more than a business where the cash flow is dependent on the owner trading his or her time or being the main technician, professional, or producer.

Recently during a 2 ½ day conference I attended as part of my affiliation with the Business Enterprise Institute, the topic was the financial reporting of a business in the various types of reports and measurements that can be used to determine how a business is actually performing. Overall, it was suggested that whatever the tools and measurements are they must be regular: weekly, monthly, quarterly, and annually.

The speaker shared that weekly you should create (translated, have created for you) reports that tell you about last week's sales, collections, bank deposits, checks written, cash on hand, cash requirements for the week, accounts receivable, accounts payable and weekly profit based on incoming cash. You should also be looking at new customer, or client leads, presentations, meetings, and things that got completed so you can track your own client acquisition costs.

The monthly review should involve a bank reconciliation and income statement so you can see how you did each and every month.

Quarterly you should meet with your financial advisor and/or CPA to review the year-to-date financials, accounts receivable, accounts payable, lines of credit, and balance sheet. In July and October, you should do a projection of your taxes and discuss potential changes to the law and to your situation with your estate planning attorney and tax planner. In March you should do a complete review of your insurance packages to make sure you are adequately covered in all areas including property and casualty, life insurance, disability insurance, and health insurance.

Annually you should hold your company meetings, including a complete review of the financials, budget, marketing, and five-year business plan. To assist you with this please see Appendix D. – Legal Audit Checklist.

Once again, with a nod towards our famous kitty cat and philosopher catcher, if you don't know where you're going, and have no method to measure whether you got there, you're guaranteed to never arrive!

PART III

THE 9 DEAL KILLERS THAT WILL WRECK THE SALE OF YOUR BUSINESS

"The race is not to the swift or the battle to the strong… but time and chance happen to them all."
ECCLESIASTES 9:11

CHAPTER SEVEN

THE 9 DEAL KILLERS[7]

"Hope is not a strategy."
RUDY GIULIANI – Mayor of New York

Here are what the Business Enterprise Institute considers to be the 9 Deal Killers that can wreck the sale of your business. Deal killers or conditions that if undetected and unresolved before the sale to a third party begins, will kill the deal. Because of this many businesses in fact end up being liquidated because a buyer cannot be found.

The good news, is you can learn how to avoid these killers. For example, think about having a business that should be worth $2,750,000 but only being able to sell it for $1,250,000. If you do not pay attention to these killers in selling your business, you may only receive half or less of what your business is actually worth.

As you read through the list, you'll notice that the first three have something in common: false assumptions. Perhaps that is why these three Killers plague so many owners who have not fully engaged in the

[7] This chapter contains information from John H. Brown, *Exit Planning, The Definitive Guide* (Business Enterprise Press 2016)

transition or exit planning process.

DEAL KILLER #1

The belief you can sell your business today for enough money to satisfy your financial independence needs and wants.

DEAL KILLER #2

The failure to reconcile your need for value with the markets perspective of the value before going to market. This involves not fully understanding the "true value" of your business.

DEAL KILLER #3

An exclusive and un-movable focus on top-line sales price.

DEAL KILLER #4

A failure to preserve and protect the company's most valuable asset – its key employees.

DEAL KILLER #5

The belief that you can negotiate a loan. More often than not, and owners first exposure to a professional buyer is often in response to an unsolicited phone call, letter or email message. The two parties agree to meet in the sale process, whether the owner realizes it or not, is underway. Buyers control the sale process in a way that reminds us of the biblical phrase, "But I was like a gentle lamb led to the slaughter." – Jeremiah 11:19

DEAL KILLER #6

An unwillingness to recruit the very best possible players for your Deal Team. We all know there are lots of professionals. We also know there are best-in-class professionals.

For example, if you wanted to pay less income taxes and could afford any CPA which would you choose: your CPA or Warren Buffett's? You need the best possible advisors to level the playing field. Using your existing advisors on your Deal Team may put you at the same disadvantage your high school basketball team would face playing the NBA All Stars.

DEAL KILLER #7

The belief that owner-initiated pre-sale due diligence isn't worth the time, effort or cost.

DEAL KILLER #8

Seller's remorse. If you feel conflicted between staying and leaving, and it is not the right time for you to go to market.

DEAL KILLER #9

Not understanding how the sales proceeds will be taxed when received. It's very important to always keep in mind that "Darth Vader" (the IRS) is also a part of any sale.

Here is a common example. John Sample owns a business as a corporation. The sale is proposed to him as a sale of assets with no assumption of liabilities. Although the sale of assets will probably be treated as long – term capital gain at the corporate level, he is not considered at all how he will get the money out of the corporation and into his hands personally. Unfortunately, however, he has already signed the Purchase and Sale Agreement without first consulting his attorney, financial advisor or accountant. How much tax will you have to pay?

The good news is you are not at the mercy of the tax system. There are a number of options that could have been considered by John on how to structure the transaction. Unfortunately, he should've had a game plan, and run the numbers on all of the various options, before he signed the Purchase and Sale Agreement. By not planning in advance, some owners have actually unintentionally structured transactions that were very adverse to them resulting for example in ordinary income tax rates rather than long – term capital gains tax rates.

I often tell clients, and a somewhat joking manner, in my opinion, the Internal Revenue Code is it really a law at all. It's a penalty system imposed on people who don't plan.

PART IV

ASSET PROTECTION PLANNING

BY RANDALL H. BORKUS

CHAPTER EIGHT

THE ASSET PROTECTION PLANNING PRIMER FOR FARMERS, RANCHERS AND BUSINESS OWNERS

Effective and decisive Asset Protection Planning is a delicate and strategic balance of the law (science) and art. The "science" or legal piece is clarity on the protections that the law provides, and the applicable statutes of your governing state jurisdiction has over your assets. The "artistic" piece is the counseling, design, crafting, application, implementation, and ongoing maintenance of the specific strategies and legal structures. You can view effective Asset Protection Planning as building a fortress with higher, thicker and wider walls around your castle with the specific goal being that those walls will be too high and too thick for an attacking creditor to climb over.

Finally, a favorite metaphor is to focus on the "three buckets" an attacking creditor and their attorneys see when they come after you, and the order in which they approach these buckets: (1) available liability insurance, (2) assets that are easy to liquidate or attach, and (3) assets that are hard or impossible to liquidate or reach through legal means. Again, effective Asset Protection Planning focuses on moving assets from bucket number two to bucket number three to the greatest extent possible.

Business owners work a lifetime to create wealth. One of the biggest risks to family wealth is lawsuits. Another risk is business failure due to a change in an industry, unforeseen liability or a downturn in the economic landscape. Asset protection planning is not for all of a business owner's assets. It is planning that generally focuses on the family "nest egg" the business owner has accumulated over time and wants to protect from the claims of creditors and predators for the benefit of the family.

Unquestionably, we would be faltering before danger if we chose to do nothing to protect our family, our wealth, our businesses and were unable to repel an assailant who threatens our family's wellbeing. In other words, everything we hold and have is His, so we have no right to just hand it over to those who would thanklessly take from us our wealth and livelihood all of which is a gift from God.

What is Asset Protection?

Asset protection is the intertwining of specific state entity, trust planning and jurisdiction planning methods to safeguard your family legacy and wealth in the event of an unforeseen creditor attack (I was hit by a Florida driver myself and got the ticket and a $2mm lawsuit), predator, divorce, medical catastrophe, business liability or some other type of personal disaster.

So we are clear, Asset Protection Planning is not about hiding assets. It is about making assets difficult, if not impossible, for creditors to reach and encumber through a court process. As a business owner you always want to be able to show your balance sheet to creditors and demonstrate how incredibly difficult it would be to reach your assets. The strategy is that you put the creditor in a no-win situation where the creditor will be forced to negotiate a reasonable settlement or just go away because it is simply too expense to pay for lawyers to pursue a judgment that has a low probability of success.

Complex asset protection planning is not appropriate for all your assets. Asset protection strategies are generally not designed to take control of assets such as your daily living expenses, mortgage payments, or loan repayments. More Accurately, asset protection planning is designed to take a portion of your wealth (your "nest egg" is what I call it), often wealth that would clearly be exposed in the event of an attack and allocate that wealth or set of assets to planning structures that would likely frustrate the efforts of future creditors. The craft of asset protection lies in moving easy to reach assets into difficult to pierce structures. The goal here is to have your family legacy beyond the reach of creditors and within reach of your family should you need to rebuild in the event of a disaster. It is not designed to shield assets that are needed for short-term or mid-term financial needs.

What are the Basic Principles of Asset Protection Planning?

One of the basic principles of asset protection planning is that you can choose which jurisdiction controls some of your your legal rights. This concept is sometimes difficult to comprehend because most of us never could choose which set of laws apply to our lives. Well, here is an instance where we have some choices.

For instance, we have no choice over who controls the transportation laws to which we all must obey. That choice is made by the municipality or state in which we are transporting, and there is no way to alter the law. Correspondingly, none of us can choose which set of tax rules apply to us in the United States. That is determined by our resident State and Federal government.

However, when it comes to our personal wealth such as personal property (ex. Securities) things we can control take a different path. The general rule is that personal property is governed by the guiding laws where the property is located. That is why the domicile or location of the owner of that property is so important. As we will see, some jurisdictions allow you to be much more protected when choosing to protect your personal property than other jurisdictions.

Do All Assets Need Special Asset Protection Planning?

Not all as states provide protective exemptions that safeguard certain assets from the reach of predators and creditors. Largely, the purpose of exemption laws is to protect certain assets or types of property so a person can continue to meet their family's basic needs and continue to earn income. These exemptions and the amounts vary greatly, depending upon the state we live in.

The types of property protected include items such as tools of the trade, jewelry within certain limitations (sometimes only an engagement ring and wedding ring), books, or a portion of the equity in an automobile. Exemptions usually protect retirement funds and qualified plans, such as IRAs, 401(k)s, and the cash value of life insurance policies. In some U.S. states only a small portion of the equity in your home is protected (The Illinois homestead exemption allows a single individual to protect up to $15,000 and $30,000 for married couples of home equity), while in other States such as Florida 100% of the equity of the primary residence is protected regardless of the value. This exemption is commonly referred to as the homestead exemption. So, prior to implementing any asset protection strategy it is important to understand the exemption laws available in your home state and how those laws impact you.

Nevertheless, if your home or cash value of your life insurance policy is protected by state law there is little reason to include it as part of an asset protection strategy.

Why Would Someone Want to Protect Their Assets From Creditors?

Life is more complicated given anyone can sue another person or entity at any time. In today's litigious society, you must assume your assets are exposed to potential creditors and predators especially if you have never sat down and thought it through with a professional planner. For farmers, ranchers, business owners and other professionals (medical, legal, accounting, engineering, or architecture), it is near impossible to foresee the financial pitfalls and liability exposures that may exist.

Even though many businesses are operated as limited partnerships, corporations or limited liability companies, all of which provide a level of personal protection from business debts, there has been a growing trend toward attaching many business liabilities to the business owner themselves. For example, business tax obligations and premises liability can attach to the owner personally, as well as liability for alleged sexual harassment and racism related claims (even if these acts were committed by an employee and not the business owner), along with a wide variety of environmental related surprises.

When you have employees and you are responsible to supervise them, you can be held liable for their bad acts or failures to act. This is particularly true when you hire someone to drive your heavy equipment, tractor trailers, farm implements and especially true for licensed professionals such as accountants, engineers, physicians, architects, dentists, real estate brokers, and attorneys.

In case where you enter contracts in your own name, rather than in the name of your business, you open the door to be sued individually when a dispute arises. When you personally guarantee a business debt, such as a commercial bank loan or when the business obtains a vendor or supplier line of credit, you are exposed to be sued individually if the bills are not paid by the business. This past year with the effects of the pandemic is a perfect example. None of us foresaw that coming and many business owners were left holding the liability bag when the business shut down and the bills were unpaid.

It is disappointing but there is no forgiveness for true accidents. When things go wrong in a personal or business situation, people have been groomed by social norms to determine who is "at fault" and then punish those who are to blame. Unfortunately, this is especially problematic for anyone who is obviously wealthy.

Though the vast majority of business owners tend to be cautious about running your day-to-day operations, you simply cannot ignore the risks you face as an owner. Therefore, it makes sense for you to meet with a professional and learn about asset protection planning options and decide what options are suitable for your situation.

The Litigation Explosion by Walter Olson does a good job of clearly laying the dramatic shift that has occurred in American's becoming the most litigious society in the world.

So, it is clear the liability exposure is a real threat but what can I do about it?

There Are Several "Building Blocks" That are Available When Asset Protection Planning. They Include:

1 Liability insurance

2 Gifting or re-titling property ownership

3 State exemption statutes

4 Use of legal entities [corporations, limited liability partnerships (LLP's) and limited liability companies (LLC's)]

5 Third-Party created Trusts

6 Domestic asset protection trusts (DAPT's)

7 International LLCs

8 International asset protection trusts

In every case I have worked on, asset protection planning involves using some combination of the building blocks.

Most business owners have begun some level of asset protection planning when they purchase liability insurance policies for automobiles, homes, office buildings, and rolling equipment. They carry forms of liability insurance, worker's compensation insurance, life insurance, disability insurance, business continuation insurance, errors and omissions (malpractice) insurance, and a minority carry a large "umbrella" liability policy.

Liability insurance is the easiest place to start creating an asset protection shield. Attacking plaintiff attorneys know this very well, and demanding policy limits is often their first focus to settle a case and get paid quickly. Easy pay days for the plaintiff's attorney often makes troubles go away quicker than you would expect. A dear friend and mentor of mine, Cecil Smith, once told me "the best approach to asset protection planning starts with determining which goat is left tied up in the front yard [for the vampires, AKA plaintiff's attorney]."

Another easy move is gifting or re-titling property into someone else's name but there is one big problem when you make a gift. The donee (recipient of the gift) now owns and controls the property and you are left without it. Notwithstanding, it may be an effective option for spouses in a strong marriage when one partner is in a risky profession (such as a physician or an attorney) to gift the primary residence or other assets in the name of their spouse.

Next, utilizing State exemption statutes are often useful to protect assets especially in the bankruptcy context. These exemptions can be complicated to understand and vary state by state. And though an exemption exists under the law there are Fraudulent transfer statutes that are in place to combat the misuse of State exemption statutes as well as other transfer. The good news is that both life insurance and annuities have some level of asset protection under most every state within certain limitations. Moreover, many states proved a homestead exemption that provides you with exemptions for your home. Florida is unlimited whereas, Illinois is limited to $15,000 per person when it comes to protecting you homestead. So, it is best to consult a licensed professional in your state regarding the use of exemption protections.

Next, utilizing the correct legal entity such as a corporation, limited liability partnership (LLP) and limited liability companies (LLC) have long been a staple when asset protection and/or tax planning. But choosing an entity form is only part of the decision. More importantly, choosing the appropriate entity jurisdiction will provide a greater asset protection shield. So, entity form coupled with the right jurisdiction creates an important combination of building blocks in your protection strategy.

Trusts created by a third parties are another solid building block option. Third-party trusts are irrevocable trusts established by one person for the benefit of others. Moreover, Third-party trusts have long been used to protect assets from creditor and predator claims. For third-party trusts to truly be effective, particular attention must be paid to drafting when weaving in the control and beneficial interests. It is imperative to work with an experienced trust attorney when enlisting Third-party trusts in your family's planning. The key to Third-party trusts is giving the trustee discretion over distributions in a way that no one can force assets to be distributed out in favor of a creditor or predator.

Next, domestic asset protection trusts (DAPTs) have become one of the most popular and versatile asset protection planning tools in the series of building blocks. Unlike the Third-party trusts, which are set up for the benefit of another, you set up a DAPT for the benefit of yourself. DAPTs are known as self-settled trusts. Several states do not allow for a self-settled trust based on the concept that it is against public policy to "create a trust for your own benefit and expect personal protection." The good news is that many states have enacted favorable DAPT laws to allow you and I to take advantage of the DAPT laws. The bottom line is DAPTs allow you to retain a personal benefit while protecting your treasured family assets and provide you a high level of asset protection. Nevertheless, DAPTs are not for everyone and to enjoy maximum confidence in your structure a domestic asset protection trust should be used in conjunction with other asset protection building blocks.

Lastly, you can consider International asset protection structures. We have all heard of using offshore asset protection trust to protect our assets from creditors and predators. One of the big problems I see with these structures is the fan fair and negative media coverage over the years. Not to mention the fact that the IRS has red flagged offshore accounts and tightened up the compliance and reporting requirements for maintaining assets offshores for all American citizens. These trusts work well yet are very complex planning tools for most families. Moreover, International planning gets very expensive very quickly and finding someone who specializes in this area of the law is complex too.

There are an overwhelming number of techniques including: Panama bearer share corporations and foundations; Switzerland and Liechtenstein annuities and trust accounts; Cook Islands, Nevis, or Belize asset protection trusts; and many more. This is a very complex area that requires an attorney and advisory team that understands these techniques. Be careful if you go this direction as these get very complicated and very expensive very quickly.

When Should I Begin Asset Protection Planning?

The best time to begin planning is when you least need it. Much like the best time to apply for a loan is when you do not need the money, and the best time to buy insurance for your boat is before you run someone over and the boat starts to sink. Simply put, you need to do this type of planning when there are no obvious threats to you or your business operations. If you wait until you have a creditor claim and then implement asset protection planning, you likely put the planning is at risk and render it ineffective.

You simply cannot protect your assets from attachment from a known creditor or current a creditor or from a "reasonably anticipated" creditor's claim. If a surgeon performs surgery on a patient and realizes sometimes later they left a scalpel inside the patent's thoracic cavity, the surgeon can anticipate a lawsuit and a future creditor claim. Asset protection planning done after the scalpel was left behind simply does not work to protect the surgeon from that inevitable lawsuit.

Obviously, the best time to begin Asset Protection Planning is before there is a problem. Planning before a harmful event occurs will also avoid a successful plaintiff allegation of a fraudulent transfer.

Why Not Just Wait to Implement Asset Protection Planning Only After You Need It?

If you wait for the problem to materialize and then move your assets to protect them, you are guaranteed a creditor will scream fraudulent conveyance or fraudulent transfer.

There are Two types of fraudulent conveyance legal arguments: actual fraud and constructive fraud. Under the law, actual fraud occurs when a debtor intentionally gifts, sells for less than fair market value or gets rid of property as part of an asset protection planning scheme after the fact. Each jurisdiction has look-back period that can be as little as one year before the filing of the bankruptcy petition, for example.

Intent to defraud must be proven for a defendant to be found guilty, but usually, certain actions are interpreted as intent, such as setting up shell corporations, scheming to retain control of transferred property, or transferring assets to an individual with whom the defendant has a relationship or tactical agreement to return the asset in the future.

Fraudulent conveyances fall under civil law, not criminal law. If the transfer of property is determined to be fraudulent, a court will require the person holding the assets (the person or entity to whom the conveyance was made) to return the assets, or an equivalent monetary value, over to the creditor.

What is interesting is that in most jurisdictions there is an assumption that after two, four or more years of moving an asset into an asset protection structure there is no intent to defraud, hinder or delay a creditor. Obviously, the best time to begin Asset Protection Planning is before you need it and then the law is on your side. "Old and cold" are the best conveyances to have made.

Is There Any Asset Protection With Joint Tenancy?

Generally, the answer is no. If the business or other assets are owned in joint tenancy, a judgment creditor can force the joint assets to be divided based upon the ownership of each joint tenant. If the business owner acquires an asset, and then transfers it to another person to be owned jointly, the creditor may be able to reach the entire value of the asset based upon a fraudulent transfer argument.

One major exception is holding real estate tenancy by the entirety. This is a special type of joint tenancy between a husband and wife only. There are twenty-six states and the District of Columbia that recognize some form of tenants by the entirety. Some states extend tenants by the entirety protection to only real estate, while other states extend it to all or nearly all assets owned jointly by husband and wife.

For example, in Illinois, married couples can only own their homestead property as tenants by the entirety. They are unable to buy and retitle investment real estate under this form of property ownership. Whereas, in Michigan, any joint tenancy previously held by a husband and wife prior to marriage converts to a tenancy by the entirety upon marriage. And then Ohio only recognizes tenancy by the entirety for deeds issued before April 4, 1985. Some states allow ownership of bank and investment accounts under tenancy by the entirety. There are no gift tax consequence for retitling to tenancy by the entirety because the unlimited federal marital deduction allows for gift tax-free transfers between spouses.

In states that recognize this concept, generally creditors of the husband or wife cannot bring an action against the asset titled tenancy by the entirety. The big exception to the tenancy by the entirety concept is if the judgment creditor has a judgment against both joint tenants. Then the asset is not protected. For example, if a home is owned by a farmer and spouse as tenants by the entirety, and the farmer gets sued for negligence, their home is safe – unless somehow the spouse was also involved in the negligent event.

Another shortcoming of tenancy by the entirety is that both tenants may need to agree to dispose of the property. So, if company stock is owned as tenants by the entirety with a husband and wife, it might be necessary that they agree on issues regarding the sale of the family business, which might not be acceptable to some business owners. Of course, if the non-debtor dies the asset that was previously protected from the creditor claims is no longer protected because the survivor now owns the entire property in his or her name alone.

If I Have a Corporation, a Limited Liability Company, or Limited Liability Partnership, Do I Have Asset Protection?

If you operate under a legal business entity, except for certain licensed professionals, your personal assets should generally be protected from business liabilities. This assumes that you follow all of the compliance rules, regulations and state filing requirements of the legal entity and have not caused yourself to otherwise be personally responsible for the business debt.

If you disregard state compliance rules and formalities that come along with owning a legal entity, you may be sued individually. For example, do you conduct annual company meetings and memorialize those meetings in the form of minutes? Do you organize these annual meetings in a minute book? If these and other required formalities are not adhered to annually and properly memorialized, it is likely that a creditor (or predator) will have the ability to "pierce your corporate veil" and hold you personally liable for the company's liabilities.

If you are a licensed professional, you are personally responsible for the acts of those that work for you and those whose activities you direct, so your corporation, LLP or LLC will provide almost no protection for your personal assets in those cases. Doctors and lawyers beware!

The concept is that your corporation, LLC or LLP are legally separate and distinct from you as the owner. However, there are cases where courts have ignored the separation of the entity and the individual and have allowed a creditor of the business to satisfy debts from the assets of the owner. This concept is known as "piercing the corporate veil."

This easiest way to avoided "piercing your corporate veil" is to abide by corporate formalities required by law such as holding annual meetings, maintaining annual and special meeting minutes, documenting items such as owner loans, salaries and all major business transactions. Also do not use the corporation's credit card or check book as your personal ATM for shopping, groceries, vacations, etc.

Unfortunately, many business owners do not think that maintaining corporate formalities is very important, so they just fail to do it. But state law requires owners follow these corporate formalities, and the results can be disastrous if ignored.

What Is The Difference Between a Limited Liability Company as Opposed To A Corporation?

The simplest example is that if the owner has a corporation, a judgment creditor can get a judicial order and take stock ownership. In the case where the business owner owns in excess of 50% of the stock, the judgment creditor could force a liquidation of the company to obtain the underlying assets to satisfy the claim.

Whereas, with a limited liability company or limited liability partnership, a creditor may only obtain a charging order. This is an order from a court that the creditor is entitled to the business owner's share of company distributions. So, if the company does not make distributions, there would be nothing for the creditor to grab. While that may not seem like much at first glance, the charging order limitation is a very powerful asset protection tool. Some states limit a creditor's rights to only a charging order. This is very powerful actually.

One theory we like is that the creditor who obtains a charging order has a right to all distributed income and is responsible for all Income

Tax on "Phantom Income" from the LLC. Example: Taxable income is not distributed and is retained in the LLC for "reasonable business purposes." Well, the charging order holder/creditor will receive a K-1 for the undistributed income. This puts the creditor in a very uncomfortable place each year they hold the charging order. Maybe they even come back to the table to negotiate their claim away.*

Sadly, in certain states a creditor can also obtain a judicial foreclosure and force a liquidation of the business, whereby the creditor would be paid. This is generally reserved for very abusive situations where a business owner formed a company for the specific purpose of defrauding a creditor in the first place.

Are Limited Liability Partnerships an Effective Asset Protection Device?

Like LLCs, the limited liability partnership can serve as an asset protection device. Like the LLC, the limited liability partnership (LLP) has charging order protection. LLPs have two classes of owners: general partners and limited partners. General partners control the business of the partnership, and generally limited partners are not involved in the operation of the business and have no say in the operations. LLPs can be effective when the intent of the business owner is to shift the majority of the ownership of the business to other family members.

* The usefulness of this approach is disputed by some professionals, but it doesn't stop us from issuing the K-1s.

A general partner can retain 1% ownership (and control), even if the limited partners own the other 99%.

The caveat here is that the general partner also has all the liability, so these structures require special planning for the general partnership ownership such as a LLC or irrevocable trust to own the general partner's share.

Again, it is critical to remember that the relative strength of any given structure varies greatly from state to state, depending on each state's applicable laws and court decisions. The LLP is useful but requires added complexity to truly protect all the partners (general and limited).

What Role Does Liability Insurance Play in Asset Protection Planning?

Liability Insurance is the first line of defense from all sorts of lawsuits. Insurance does not avoid liability but provides a source of funds to defend you and pay a judgment against you for damages.

The real dilemma is "how much is enough?" And what type of liability insurance? As a general rule you must have an umbrella policy which is also referred to as excess liability coverage policy. These policies are generally inexpensive and make good sense. This type of policy will increase the general liability limits of the existing liability and property insurance policies for a specific amount.

One risk is that the umbrella insurance limits start at an amount higher than the underlying liability and property insurance policy. This can create a "gap" in coverage and often occurs when there are different insurance companies involved. So, if you obtain an umbrella policy, it is important to be sure the coverage starts where the underlying policy limits stop.

Also, if there is insurance it is important to be sure that the right insured is named. While this may seem obvious, many business owners will transfer ownership of assets or businesses to various entities, or form new entities, and forget to advise their insurance representative of changes. Thus, the insurance company may allege that there is no coverage for a claim where the wrong individual or company is named as insured. If there are multiple companies, it may be necessary to name the subsidiary companies as additional insureds on policies, so that all of the entities are covered.

It's also important that you're clear on exactly what the insurance covers. Certain acts or events may not be covered unless there is a specific endorsement. An example would be an endorsement for gender or sexual harassment or acts of discrimination. These are not covered by the typical liability policy. If you have many employees, this is an endorsement you should consider.

Also, many policies will not cover theft of personal information and electronic information, nor damage to documents. Specific endorsements are attainable for these risks.

What If The Lawsuit is Alleging Damages In Excess of the Policy Limits?

If a lawsuit is for an amount in excess of the policy limits, the business owner is at risk. Many lawsuits do not specifically state an amount that is sought initially. So, even if there is insurance coverage, and the insurance company is defending the lawsuit, the business owner may want to retain his or her own attorney to defend the lawsuit. Of course, hiring an attorney for this purpose can be quite expensive but this possibility buttresses the argument for combining asset protection strategies.

Can I Just Give Away My Assets?

You can but do you really want to just give your assts away? Really? In most cases, it does not work to simply give away assets or simply change the ownership and titling. Remember, the Fraudulent transfer and conveyance laws provide that if someone transfers assets with the intent to hinder, delay, or defraud a creditor those assets transferred will be brought back. As discussed above, these transfers are referred to as fraudulent conveyances or fraudulent transfers.

An exception would be for transfers of assets that are not otherwise subject to the claims of creditors and are exempt under the applicable state laws. Likewise, the transfer of an asset for full and adequate consideration (fair market value) should not be considered a fraudulent conveyance. On the other hand, transfers whereby the business owner becomes insolvent will be deemed a fraudulent conveyance. Conversely, a transfer whereby the business owner is not insolvent after the transfer should not be considered a fraudulent conveyance.

The trouble with fraudulent conveyances is that there is no way to get inside the mind of the business owner to know what precipitated the transfer. What has evolved in the law is the concept of "badges of fraud." Actions that suggest a fraudulent transfer include such things as a conveyance to a relative, a conveyance in anticipation of a lawsuit, a transfer of all or nearly all of a debtor's property, leaving them unable to pay debts after the transfers.

If a fraudulent transfer occurs, a creditor can ask the court to set aside or reverse the transfer, to allow the creditor to execute against the asset that was transferred, to prevent future transfers of the property, and go so far as to appoint an independent third party to take charge of the assets (often referred to as a receiver). Further, advisors and attorneys that advise the business owner to engage in fraudulent activities can be guilty of criminal behavior in some states.

What are Asset Protection Trusts?

Asset Protection Trusts are irrevocable trusts that are established by a business owner for his or her own benefit (referred to as "self-settled") and may also be for the benefit of his or her spouse and family members. The trust is a discretionary trust, that is, no one can compel the trustee to make distributions as the trustee holds the sole discretion to make or not make distributions of trust assets. Asset Protection Trusts have what is referred to as a "spendthrift provision" that prohibits the trustees and beneficiaries of the trust from pledging the assets of the trust as collateral, assigning the assets, or encumbering the assets in any way.

With a spendthrift provision, the trust property is generally not subject to legal process or to the claims of any creditors while it remains trust property. If these trusts are set up in the United States they are referred to as domestic asset protection trusts (DAPTs), as opposed to trusts set up in other countries which are referred to as foreign asset protection trusts or offshore trusts.

As of this writing, seventeen states allow for self-settled Domestic Asset Protection Trusts ("DAPTs"). Those states are Alaska, Delaware, Hawaii, Michigan, Mississippi, Missouri, Nevada, New Hampshire, Ohio, Oklahoma, Rhode Island, South Dakota, Tennessee, Utah, Virginia, West Virginia, and Wyoming.

Generally, the business owner cannot oversee or control the trust, or a court could conclude that the business owner retained too much control over the trust assets. An independent trustee such as a bank or trust company is often the best choice though states like South Dakota, Nevada and Wyoming have what is known as a private family trust company. A private family trust company is a statutory qualified trustee which means the trustee duties can be governed by a family board with the assistance of an independent third-party manager.

It is important to remember that Asset Protection Trusts do not avoid the challenges involving fraudulent transfers. So, again, it is best to establish these trusts before the business owner has any problems. Some states have 2-year, 4-year and 6-year look-back periods as how long must transpire before an asset transfer is assumed not made to defraud, hinder or delay a creditor.

Alas, in 2005 Congress amended the Bankruptcy Code and created a 10-year limitations or look-back period for transfers to self-settled trusts. This means that transfers to DAPTs will be suspect for the 10-years prior to the date that a federal bankruptcy petition is filed. Thus, this makes domestic asset protection trusts more riskier if your plan was to file bankruptcy. Still, this also underscores the need to plan well in advance to a problem occurring. If more than ten years pass before a bankruptcy petition is filed, the assets in a DAPT should not be at risk. Alternatively, if you are in a court of equity and not bankruptcy you would be subject to the states have 2-year, 4-year and 6-year look-back period after which it is assumed no fraudulent intent.

It must be said that outside of bankruptcy, the IRS may have a super-priority over DAPTs and spendthrift trusts. The typical asset protection afforded by a DAPT against creditor claims, may not hold up when the creditor is the IRS. Note in some states claims for unpaid child support are not protected by a DAPT.

Can Other Trusts, Such as My Revocable Living Trust, Be Used for Asset Protection?

Revocable living Trusts established by the business owner during their lifetime will not provide any asset protection for the business owner. I have had countless clients tell me their financial advisor told them that a revocable living trust provides them with asset protection. That is simply NOT TRUE!

However, when a revocable living trust is properly drafted on behalf of your beneficiaries after you are gone, it will provide a high level of third-party trust protection for your beneficiaries.

Like anything else when you are building something you need a strong foundation. So, at a minimum a business owner should establish a foundational estate plan that utilizes revocable living trusts for themselves and then for the benefit of their beneficiaries.

A separate share trust for the benefit of your heirs that is established at your death, and contains a spendthrift provision, provides some of the strongest protection available from the claims of creditors. Moreover, proper drafting of these third-party created trusts (separate shares under a revocable living trust) for your beneficiaries can protect the trust assets from creditors and predators and from a beneficiary's divorcing spouse. This is important in this era where over 50% of all marriages end up in divorce. We would never wish this to happen to our children or grandchildren; but it is much better to have divorce protection as well as creditor and predator protection built into your foundational estate plan for your beneficiaries.

Do I Avoid Paying Income Taxes When I Have an Asset Protection Trust?

Asset protection trusts whether domestic or international do not save you any income taxes as they are "tax neutral." The general rule is that U.S. residents are subject to taxation on their worldwide income. The fact that assets are in a foreign asset trust does not change this obligation for U.S. citizens. Although some unscrupulous promoters of Foreign Asset Protection Trusts advise their clients that they can hide offshore income from the IRS and avoid paying tax, they are wrong. It is against the law for a U.S. citizen to commit the felony of Tax Evasion. Whereas Tax Avoidance, or tax planning is legal. When asked "What's the biggest difference between Tax Avoidance and Tax Evasion?" The answer is 20 years in federal prison.

Do I Still Have to Carry Liability Insurance Once an Asset Protection Trust is in Place?

Absolutely, remember it is about putting up building blocks, so first liability insurance then the asset protection trust. One of the important aspects of liability insurance is the insurance company's obligation to defend the policyholder in litigation. That in itself is reason enough to continue carrying liability insurance policy. You also want to insure against the risk of loss of personal wealth that is not protected in the asset protection trust.

What About Offshore or International Asset Protection Planning?

There are several types of planning structures available internationally for asset protection, depending on the jurisdiction.

Traditionally, the most popular jurisdictions for offshore planning include Nevis, the Cook Islands, Liechtenstein, the Isle of Mann, Jersey, and Gibraltar. It is very important to ensure that the jurisdiction has statutory authority to allow you to be a beneficiary of any trust you create (known as a "self-settled trust"). Moreover, the jurisdiction must be politically and economically stable, and have its legal roots well-grounded in English common law.

One of the most common international structures is the transfer of assets to an international entity (typically a limited liability company) and a subsequent transfer of the limited liability company ownership to an international trust. The underlying assets rarely leave the United States; yet, the assets are titled in the name of the new international entity. There are also numerous tax and reporting compliance requirements which make this complex. Therefore, know that international planning should not be undertaken without experienced professional assistance.

Using international law to supercharge an asset protection plan has a lot of advantages and U.S. court cases have confirmed these structures work. Again, it is important to understand that international asset protection is not about income tax planning or tax evasion. The structure is income tax neutral.

Additionally, this is not about hiding assets; instead, it is about creating solid building blocks, so you become an undesirable defendant to a creditor or "predator."

The advantages of using international planning include:

1. International courts in many countries are not required to recognize the judgments from other countries.
2. Foreign countries often require a shorter look-back period after transfering assets.

3. Most foreign jurisdictions have a presumption against fraudulent transfers rather than an assumption that there was a fraudulent transfer.
4. Most foreign jurisdictions require a higher standard of proof for a judgment.
5. Some foreign jurisdictions provide that even if a part of a transfer is determined to be fraudulent then the trust will still remain intact.

There are also added attorney fees for creditors and few attorneys are licensed internationally, so a plaintiff must hire local counsel. Many jurisdictions require that attorneys may bill only hourly rates (rather than getting 30-40 percentage of a judgement). This greatly disincentivizes attorneys from putting forth great effort only to earn an hourly wage so this helps to reduce the "Lottery Syndrome" that drives so much litigation in the U.S.! Additionally, many foreign jurisdictions require posting a substantial bond (sometimes tens of thousands of dollars) to even begin a lawsuit.

All these hurdles are highly effective in making a creditor plaintiff think twice before attempting to go after an international asset protection plan. In many cases, they are more likely to accept the limits of a liability insurance policy, or other settlement that is being offered.

Can Real Estate Assets Be Protected With an Offshore Asset Protection Trust?

Generally, the answer is that it is difficult to predict. Keep in mind that the underlying premise of the planning involves moving ownership of property to an offshore entity that is not bound by U.S. court decisions. While real estate can be owned in an offshore entity, the real property itself is still in the United States. Therefore, real property is theoretically within the domain of the state court where the real property is located. Therefore, you do not completely remove real estate from the jurisdiction of U.S. courts, and U.S. judges will feel no restraint in issuing judgments involving liens on U.S. real estate.

However, if the real estate has been owned for a long time by an asset protection structure, (well past the look-back period) the probability of protection is greatly improved with time. There is something to be said about "old and cold" planning that has been completed years earlier.

Where Do the Assets Reside if They Are Contributed to a Foreign Asset Protected Structure?

There is a lot of misunderstanding about where assets in an asset protection planning strategy are kept. Some people have misgivings about having their assets reside overseas, and most advisors would not suggest that you put your assets in the hands of a stranger.

Maintaining control and enjoyment of your assets is a cornerstone of any planning. The good news is that your assets can continue to be held in a U.S. financial institution, most often with your existing financial advisor. The key is that control of those assets resides with a professional trustee in a foreign country that has favorable asset protection laws. Therefore, the assets physically reside in the U.S. financial institution of your choice.

So What is the Cost of Foreign Asset Protection Planning?

As with all planning, there is an initial cost for due diligence, design, and implementation. Offshore planning will also require ongoing trustee and other maintenance fees. Additionally, there are annual costs to monitor, maintain, and update any asset protection plan. It is safe to say that all asset protection strategies involve some cost, even if the only cost is the payment of liability insurance premiums. There are no free rides.

For clients using trusts and limited liability companies or limited liability partnerships in their estate planning already, the cost of most asset protection enhancements are minimal to the overall planning fees. However, to complete the best planning in complex cases, working in a collaborative fashion with experts will be required. Each case is different and therefore, the cost is something to discuss in advance with your advisory team.

So What is the Cost of Ignoring Asset Protection Planning?

Woefully, many folks who failed to commit to asset protection planning can testify that the cost of NOT doing the planning is exponentially higher than any fees they would have spent for the protection in the first place.

Asset Protection Planning Specific to Farmers and Ranchers and Land Holders

The biggest challenge for most farm and ranch families is the same. "How do we keep the real estate in the family for generations?"

Whether it's a farm, or a ranch or another form of income producing real estate, the goal of most families is the same; keep the assets in the family bloodline for generations.

The first concept in achieving this ultimate goal, is to understand that "fair" and "equal" does not always mean the same thing.

It's not unusual for a family of four or six children to have the majority of them go to college and not return to farm. The problem this creates is the ones who stay behind to dedicate their life's to farming can be left with a huge burden when in the end they are responsible to work the farm the rest of their life without the assistance of the other siblings.

For example, I've seen where four out of six siblings went off to college and got wonderful education and jobs which had them settled in four different places in the United States. Each was 1000 or more miles away from the family farm. Meanwhile, one brother and one sister, went to college and focused on agricultural degrees. They returned to the farm to spend their life working. After spending 15 to 20 years of their life's working with the parents to make a successful business, the parents died. There was no formal plan in place as dad always said the kids would figure it out between them. Or equally disheartening, it was discovered that the parents left behind simple wills, which left everything to their children equally.

The two siblings who worked the farm found themselves in one of three situations, all of which destroy the family legacy and was financially destructive.

Situation #1 – The two siblings were required to share two-thirds of their income with the non-farming siblings, which meant that they could not afford to continue farming so they just sold everything.

Situation #2 - The two siblings were required to leverage the farm to pay off the other siblings and spend the rest of their lives in debt to pay off the other siblings.

Situation #3 - There was no income to distribute to the non-farm siblings effectively blowing up the family dynamic and forcing the sale of the farm.

In every case above, family dynamic blows up and after years and years of emotional discord and distrust, led to extensive litigation, breaking up the family farm into six separate shares and destroying the family for generations.

This is a perfect example of fair and equal not being the same thing.

Many rural country attorneys are very good at probate and real estate transactions but may only touch on estate and succession planning on a part-time basis. I run into families who have been sold on the idea that real estate ownership can be segregated or broken up into lifetime interest and remainder interests and nothing more. This can cause serious complications when it comes time to pass on those treasured assets to the next generation.

For example, the lifetime interest gives the holder (mom and dad) the right to enjoy the land during their lifetime and provides a degree of asset protection for mom and dad as lifetime liabilities against them personally will not extend to the remainder interest in the land, in most cases, which is typically held by the children.

I have seen this planning backfire multiple times now with farm and ranch families. For example, when a child holds a remainder interest in their individual name that gives them certain legal rights as well as liability considerations. The parents who hold the lifetime interest are not allowed to sell any of the land without the agreement and signatures of the remainder interest holders (the children). Another consequence of the remainder interest being held by the children is that any of the children's personal liability can give a creditor the right to put a lien against the real estate, farm or ranch. I have literally seen this play out when a family went to sell a section and they come to find out their youngest son had an outstanding personal liability of almost $100,000 that needed to be satisfied before they could consummate the sale. This created a high level of family discourse and that child was partially disinherited by the parents.

Another issue I have witnessed is where the family lawyer advised the remainder interest be gifted to the children who would be ultimately transfer their remainder interests to a family limited liability partnership. In this case, mom and dad gifted a remainder interest in the family farm which had been in the bloodline for 125 years. They had the land appraised and there was a calculation of the value of the remainder interest, and they filed gift tax returns. It seems on its face that there was some thoughtful estate planning and asset protection planning put in place, but it fell short when one of the siblings died prematurely and their spouse of less than one year was in line to inherit 1/3 of the family farm.

It got worse, as under the partnership agreement there was some draconian language that required the partnership or the other partners to exercise a right to purchase the interest of a deceased partner. The partnership agreement specifically stated that the deceased partners interest in the partnership would not be subject to any discount in value for lack of marketability, or lack of control.

Moreover, the deceased sibling did not have a personal estate plan in place, so the bride of 11 months affectively received cash equivalent to 1/3 interest remainder interest in the family farm. This was never the intent of the family let alone that they needed to leverage the family farm to the tune of $750,000.00 to pay off the DECEASED siblings estate (AKA "spouse").

Losing a sibling was devastating enough for this family, and now they will need to work to pay down this $750,000 mortgage. In the eyes of the family, this planning completely failed, and it literally cost them over $750,000 because the estate planning piece was not thoroughly thought through.

To make matters worse, in that same case, mom and dad had gifted a quarter of land directly to the deceased sibling when they made the original remainder interest gifts. The quarters of farmland is now owned by the spouse of 11 months. Yet another blow to the family. All totaled, the family spent about $10,000 on the original planning and it ended up costing them in excess of $1 million of family wealth due to the lack of vision and poor planning from the professional whom the family trusted.

This is a perfect example of where my Bloodline Preservation Trust℠* or a Family Legacy Trust could have been used to protect the family farm and ensure the farmland stayed in the bloodline for generations.

It is not uncommon for a family in a similar situation to pay attorney fees in excess of $50,000 to ensure a multi-generational legacy. In the bigger picture, the family who spent the $50,000 for bloodline preservation trust planning not only saves a $1 million mistake described above, but they also ensured smooth transition of the family farm or real estate business. This also keeps the family from being traumatized by finding out the original planning their parents had done failed them miserably.

So much of what we look at when we are considering asset protection planning is for the individual; however, wise families who step up and do their advanced estate planning also create an asset protection structure for the next generation and multiple generations to follow.

Family estate planning disasters are not limited to farm or ranch families. A very successful oil field family business bought and sold oil gas and mineral interests for a couple of generations. When the second generation took the business over, they thought it appropriate to start gifting interest in these mineral properties to the third generation, and not report these gifts as required under the U.S. tax code. The short version of this story is they created a public paper trail of ownership

* See appendix C.

changes and the cash flow changes as these properties went from the second generation to the third generation. Generation two was convinced that the IRS would be unable to detect the transfers.

After the second generation died, the third generation spent hundreds of thousands of dollars in legal fees and millions of dollars in gift taxes, estate tax and penalties and interest associated with the undocumented illegal gift transfers. This is another case of the second generation was unwilling to spend anything in legal fees over their lifetime to properly transfer ownership of multiple millions of dollars of properties. There is no question, that proper gift planning over a lifetime would have saved the family millions of dollars and saved them from anguish in the public shaming of the previous generation's foolishness.

The story is not quite over yet, as a few years after the fight with the IRS one of the siblings in generation three filed for a divorce to find out that they would lose 50% of their wealth in the divorce settlement. This is yet another area where a bloodline preservation plan would have protected the family legacy asset.

There are cases and cases of families that either planned poorly or not at all. Or one sibling assumed he or she knew how the assets were structured and found out it was not actually what was legally true. There are multiple forms of Bloodline Preservation Trust℠ or a Family Legacy Trusts, some that benefit spouses, some of that benefit spouses and children and some that only benefit children.

CLOSING STORY

The following story shared by Bruce Wright in his incredible book, The Wright Exit Strategy.

> *"Picture a courtroom, if you will, where a lawsuit has been filed against a professional. You, the plaintiff, are claiming malfeasance of some nature. You're telling the judge, "my advisor didn't look out for my best interests. She messed this up and it cost me X amount of money. She should've known that these investments were not suitable for me. She should have known that this particular tactic or tool was going to expose me to an undue level of risks which I could not tolerate." The attorney for the defense approaches you and says, "perhaps you can tell the court what your goals and objectives are. Perhaps you can articulate that for us." If you can't articulate your own goals and objectives, you can have a pretty difficult time winning your case. If you don't know what it is, you're doing, where you are, where you want to go and how you want to get there, it's pretty ridiculous to think that you could hire a professional, pay her X amount of money and expect her to read your mind and guess right and all these important issues.*
>
> *I met with the father and son who were trying to buy out the family agriculture business from the dad's two sisters. Their accountant had done a beautiful overview of how they should go about this*

transaction. Our firm was hired to give a second opinion and review all of the information, to make sure all the T's were crossed and the I's were doubted. I looked at the strategic plan put forward by the accountant and I thought, "this is fabulous. This is one of the most articulate, in – depth plans I've ever seen. I would actually outsource some work to that accounting firm." It was done that well. I told everybody that when we all got together. The clients, the accountant and the financial advisors were all happy to hear what a great plan they had in front of them.

When we all sat down in the financial advisor's office, I said, "this is a great overview. The T's crossed in the I's are dotted and everything is ready to go. I just have a few questions for you."

I looked over at the data and asked, "if you could just get a check in the mail every month, how much total annual income after taxes do you think you would be able to live uncomfortably for the rest of your life?"

He said, "Well, I would need about $75,000 a year." I asked the son the same question and he said $125,000 a year. I asked the father what his net worth was and he said it was about $6 million most of it tied up in the family agriculture business. The son's net worth was about $4 million most of it again tied up in the family agriculture business. Next, I asked, "If you could create the perfect calendar and you could live the lifestyle you really want; if you could spend your time, talent and resources doing exactly what you want to do, whenever you want to do it; if you could get rid of all *the activities that you don't want to do, what would that perfect calendar look like?"*

They leanded back in their chairs, and the dad said, "Well, I never really thought about that before." "Well, give it some thought," I told them, "What, really important things would you like to do with your time, talent and resources?"

So, we started listing some of their key activities. Finally, I asked them both, "Is there anything missing? Anything that isn't on the list?" They said, "No, we don't think so. We got all the big things, anyway."

I said, "Okay, it's kind of hard to answer that question all at one time. But how about spending 70 hours a week running an agriculture business? I don't see that on the list for your perfect calendar." The dad said, "Well, you said if it was the perfect calendar and we could do whatever we wanted to do."

I said, "Yes, that's the question I ask."

And then the son got it. It was like watching a cartoon with a light bulb going on over his head. He looked at his dad and said, "dad, we've got to get on the same page. We're not really living the lives we want to live. We've got everything tied up in the business and what we're about to do is take our $10 million of net worth, pledged as collateral and borrow another $20 million so we can buy out Aunt Sylvia and Aunt Mary. The point is, we could be living our perfect calendar if we got out of the business too."

The father said, "I never thought of that. I thought I was just going to work at the business until I died." At this point the accountant joined the conversation. He said to the son, "You mentioned that we need to be on the same page. We are on the same page. In fact, you have 50 pages of analysis, recommendations and summary of the same page." The accountant was noticeably irritated with the clients, and with the direction of the conversation and with me.

As lovingly as possible, I reaffirmed the fine job he and his firm had done. Then I pointed out that there was only one problem with the analysis: the accountant and let the client incorrectly define the mission. This is an all-too-common problem with the communication between clients and advisers. Clients don't always know what the real questions or right issues are. But the client defines the issues as well as the advisor's role and together they march right down the wrong path.

What I am offering is a new paradigm is this: let's get on this right page. You must make sure that you and the people you work with are on the "right page" and moving in the best direction for you the left brained financial analysis offered by the accountant had not taken into account the critical right brain issues necessary to move the clients to a higher level of fulfillment and quality of life"

Thank you very much Bruce for this great story and tremendous example of what it is he were trying to accomplish here. And for you dear reader the next time I see Bruce I'll thank him on behalf of both of us.

AFTERWORD

We admit it. Our principal purpose in writing this book was somewhat selfish. We were frustrated and tired of watching too many business owners fail to take full advantage of the last act in their business careers simply because they lack information and guidance. Writing this book – with no other agenda than to educate owners – is our way of dealing with our frustration. With this book, we hope you now have enough information to begin, tackle, and successfully transition or exit from your business.

As with everything we do our law firms, finding the balance between enough and too much information is a constant battle. The danger in providing too much information is that you toss this book aside, too overwhelmed to even begin to plan. With too little information, you would join the many owners who don't realize there is in fact much that can be done, and likely must be done, if you are too leave your business when you want, with the money you need, with the minimum amount of taxes, and in the capable hands of your chosen successor. Hopefully have found the sweet spot between these two and you are at least persuaded that planning your transition or exit is a task well worth your time and energy.

That being said, we suspect you may also be thinking to yourself, "How in the heck am I ever going to find the time and energy to plan for, initiate, and execute a comprehensive transition or exit plan and still do everything that's necessary to keep my business running well?" What a great question!

Yes, of course, in order to create a successful transition or exit you must set and prioritize goals, analyze your gap, install and fortify value drivers, pick the right transition or exit path. Design the transfer to minimize your risk and keep you in control all the while making sure your family is secure if you don't make it to the finish line. The good news, is you do not have to do this all alone. This book is merely a short guidebook, not a self – help or how – to book for the simple reason that no business owner, in our opinion at least, is capable of designing and implementing a transition or exit plan alone. The other obvious reality is that no one advisor can do it all either.

If you have completed this book, congratulations! Hopefully you highlighted the information and ideas that jumped out at you, scribbled in the pages, and dogeared some of the pages. Having done that, you are on your way to the transition or exit planning future that you desire. Your next task is to find someone to lead your team; someone trained in the transition or exit planning process we've described in this book. A great place to start is taking a few minutes to do the Assessment contained in appendix B.

It's very possible that one of your current advisors (especially if one gave you this book) has that training and experience. On the other hand, if you attempt to create your own transition or exit plan or work with advisers who has little or none of this type of experience, and make one guarantee: You will spend valuable time, endless energy, and too much money for little, if any, positive result.

The exciting news is that with a successful transition or exit you can leave a legacy and not just a job. Please use this book as a basic outline or blueprint to help you work with your advisors to create a plan, leave your business in good hands, reward yourself and your family for years of effort, and leave the rest of your life in a way that gives it meaning.

All that being said, can we encourage you to turn the page and take a look at Appendix A discussing who we are as a law firm, what exactly is it that we do, and what makes us different. We would love and be honored to have the opportunity to help you.

All the best!

APPENDIX A

HELPING YOU TRANSITION OR EXIT

What We Do and How We Are Different

What We Do

Exit or Transition Business Planning

We are very proud and excited to be affiliated with the Business Enterprise Institute and we diligently and thoroughly follow the 7 Step Exit Planning Process created, monitored, and taught by BEI.

Business Planning

For example, what type of business entity is best for you to use

(Corporation, LLC, partnership, etc.). Confidentiality agreements and general business advice including employee issues, Non—compete agreements, and tax advice.

Wealth Protection Planning

These services include both basic foundational and advanced estate planning, insurance and liability planning, asset protection planning, and family advice.

How We Are Different

Our goal is to goal is to Co-Create a comprehensive Family Wealth Protection Plan, or business Transition or Exit Plan, that will actually work with people who care.

Yes, you have to invest time, energy, emotion and money. However, it will produce peace of mind for you and protection for your family or business.

No Law Firm can be an expert in everything. The focus of our practice's wealth and personal protection for families and individuals and smooth transition or exit planning for business owners. What makes us unique is our membership into national organizations. The Wealth Counsel nationwide organization of estate planning attorneys for families and individuals; and, the Business Enterprise Institute on the business owner side.

The mission of both of these organizations is quite simple...." It doesn't work for the client, it doesn't work."

In working with us you're not going to find perfection. What you will find is a law firm that deals with difficult life, disability, death, and business succession issues on a regular basis which has produced exceptional results people did not think were possible.

There are other ways to do this planning. For example, using a general practice law firm or trying to do it yourself on the computer. The real question is willing those other ways produce a plan that actually works when you need it or not?

Our mission is to reduce, and in some cases eliminate your anxieties, fears, and concerns about the future. We actually help people act in their own best interests. "Peace of mind, not just piece of paper."

The key question to ask yourself is, "If I decide to invest the time, emotion, energy, and money to create a Family Wealth Protection Plan, or a Business Transition/Exit Plan, what's in it for me?"

APPENDIX B

GOALS ASSESSMENT

The foundation of all of your planning should be your goals. The writing of your transition or exit plan begins here as you set forth your initial goals. As you work through the exercises, questions, and counseling sessions with us, it's likely that you will return to clarify, refine, and prioritize whatever you right here.

You, your family, and your advisors will refer to your goals often as you plan and implement decisions along the path of your eventual transition or exit.

Financial Independence

What amount of cash must you have in order to exit? Express this annual pretax income you need for the rest of your, and your spouse, or partners lives. ____________________

A Are you willing to exit or transition from your business – transfer ownership and control – without the assurance of financial security?

☐ Yes ☐ No

B When you have more time and freedom after you leave the business, will you spend less money?

☐ Yes ☐ No

C What post-exit activities will you and your spouse or partner enjoy, and how much will these activities cost? ____________________

How will you determine, with precision, what you need?____________________

Financial Wants

How much cash do you want to live a financially comfortable and long post – exit life?

A Once you know you can exit or transition from your business and meet your financial independence needs, will you continue to own the business until you can also satisfy all of your financial wants?

☐ Yes ☐ No

B Do you want your family to receive this level of income if you don't survive?

☐ Yes ☐ No

Departure Date

How long must you work in your business to achieve financial security as well as your universal and aspirational goals?

Consider, for a moment, your exit or transition date.

A Do you want to work until your children reach a certain age or education level?

B Do you want to work until your business reaches a certain value?

C When are you think of leaving the business in_____years?

D What does "leaving" or "exiting" the business mean to you?

- ☐ A specific timeframe
- ☐ A reduced level of physical, mental or emotional involvement in the business
- ☐ No longer having to think about the things you don't want to think about or do
- ☐ Beginning to transfer or sell some ownership before you depart and before control is transferred
- ☐ Getting out entirely. Having no ownership or involvement in the business

Questions To Ponder

A if you could leave the business sooner, would you?

☐ Yes ☐ No

B if, today, I offered you enough cash for your business to provide you with financial security/financial independence, would you take it immediately and exit?

☐ Yes ☐ No

Desired Successor

A My chosen successor is:

1 ____

2 A third-party________________________________

3 These family members___________________________

4 These members of my management team_______________

B Do you have a strong preference for one type of successor over another?

1 One of the reasons behind your preference?_______________

2 If there were a way for your key people to acquire the needed skills and the money to buy you out, would you consider them as possible successors?

☐ Yes ☐ No

3 If your chosen successor chooses not to succeed you do you have a backup?

☐ Yes ☐ No

APPENDIX C

KEEPING IT IN THE FAMILY – BLOODLINE PRESERVATION TRUST℠

BY RANDALL H. BORKUS © 2004-2021

An irrevocable trust set up by someone other than one of the beneficiaries provides the ultimate in creditor protection. With a divorce rate of over 50%, as well as an increasing number of personal lawsuits, creditor protection is often the most important objective of our planning clients.

The creator of a Bloodline Preservation Trust℠ can dictate who may receive the beneficial enjoyment of the property and the extent and circumstances under which this enjoyment continues. As a result, unless trust property is distributed outright to a beneficiary, it will generally be protected from the beneficiary's creditors so generally the Bloodline Preservation Trust℠ principal is not distributed, only the income.

For mature, competent family members who would receive the property outright were it not for the benefits that can be derived through the receipt of property in a trust, the trust should be designed to give the beneficiary of a trust the functional equivalent of outright ownership, including undisturbed control over the property. Many candidates for this type of planning would be unwilling to create such a structure unless the trust benefits are coupled with the Bloodline Preservation Trust℠ of the beneficiary to obtain control over the trust property that is virtually tantamount to outright ownership.

In order to achieve the maximum transfer tax savings, the Bloodline Preservation Trust℠ should be wholly exempt from the generation-skipping transfer tax. This will avoid the imposition of transfer taxes for successive generations. The Bloodline Preservation Trust℠ should be drafted as a dynasty trust when possible which is an irrevocable trust that is protected from estate taxes for as long as applicable state law allows. With proper drafting, a Bloodline Preservation Trust℠ can also be designed to protect the trust assets from the creditors and divorcing spouses of the trust beneficiaries. Many of our farmer/rancher clients and large real estate investing clients demand these protections.

The Bloodline Preservation Trust℠ concept is that if it makes sense to protect the trust assets from creditors and estate taxes at the first generational level, then the identical notion should apply at the next generation and each generation after for the longest time period allowable by state law. Since the primary beneficiary at each generation can be given control in some cases over the trust, there should be no reason to ever draft a irrevocable trust without making it a Bloodline Preservation Trust℠.

Support Trusts vs. Discretionary Trusts

A Bloodline Preservation Trust℠ can be drafted as either a "support trust" or a "pure discretionary trust" for creditor protection purposes. The pure discretionary Bloodline Preservation Trust℠ is more complex, but exponentially more protective than a support version of the Bloodline Preservation Trust℠.

A support trust is created by the grantor to support one or more beneficiaries for the beneficiary's lifetime. A support trust directs the trustee to distribute the trust's income and/or principal as is necessary for the support of a beneficiary. The beneficiary of a support trust can, in some cases, induce the trustee to make a distribution of trust income or principal merely by demonstrating that the money is necessary for the beneficiary's maintenance, education or healthcare, or whatever other standard the grantor wishes to create in the trust. The standard for distributions often contains words such as "health, education, and maintenance" since that language keeps the trust assets outside of the trustee/beneficiary's estate even though that person is both a beneficiary and in rare cases the trustee.

A discretionary Bloodline Preservation Trust℠ allows the trustee complete and uncontrolled discretion to make allocations of income or principal if and when the trustee deems appropriate. Because the trustee is given such broad powers, the beneficiary can only compel the trustee to distribute funds if it can be shown that the trustee is abusing its discretion by failing to act in the beneficiary's best interest, acting dishonestly, or acting with an improper purpose in regard to the motive in denying the beneficiary the funds sought.

A discretionary Bloodline Preservation Trust℠ generally uses permissive language such as the word "may" instead of the word "shall." The permissive word "may" is still generally further qualified by granting the trustee autonomous discretion using words such as "sole and absolute discretion," "absolute and uncontrolled discretion," or "sole, absolute discretion and unreviewable."

Spendthrift Provisions

A spendthrift provision is a provision in a trust agreement that states that the beneficiary cannot sell, pledge or encumber his beneficial interest, and that a creditor cannot attach a beneficiary's interest. At common law, the purpose of a spendthrift trust was to protect a beneficiary from his own spending habits. The idea was to provide for someone who could not provide for himself, and to keep such beneficiary from becoming dependent on public assistance. Therefore, if a spendthrift clause was added to a trust, the common law developed a legal principle that a creditor could not recover from the beneficiary's interest.

A beneficiary of discretionary Bloodline Preservation Trust℠ does not need to rely on a spendthrift provision because neither the current distribution interest nor any subsequent interest is a property interest under state law. Therefore, neither the beneficiary nor the creditors of the beneficiary have any right to force a distribution from the Bloodline Preservation Trust℠. However, seasoned trust scriveners always include spendthrift provisions even when using a discretionary Bloodline Preservation Trust℠

Conclusion

It is generally deficient to draft a Bloodline Preservation Trust℠ or any other trust with mandatory staggered distributions for the beneficiaries upon reaching certain ages. Rather, the trust should be drafted to continue in trust for the beneficiary's protection from predators and their future decisions. For maximum creditor and divorce protection, the trust should be designed as a discretionary trust rather than a support trust as the goal is to protect assets for generations.

APPENDIX D

WHAT IS YOUR FAVORITE ASSET PROTECTION PLANNING TOOL?

My favorite asset protection planning tool is a combination or tools. I call it the "Ultimate Cowboy Cocktail". The Ultimate Cowboy Cocktail" refers to Wyoming's "multi-barreled" approach to asset protection. It is a Wyoming Domestic Asset Protection Trust (WYDAPT), a Wyoming Close Limited Liability Company (LLC) and a Wyoming "Private Family Trust Company" (PTC) combination that provides a strong asset protection structure.

Wyoming is one of a minority of states that offers self-settled domestic asset protection trust statutes. A WYDAPT is an irrevocable trust, known as a "spendthrift" trust, and is set up to meet your particular asset protection goals. A grantor or creator of a WYDAPT may be a beneficiary of the trust under Wyoming statute. WYDAPT may also be created by a parent/grantor who fears that their children are "spendthrifts"

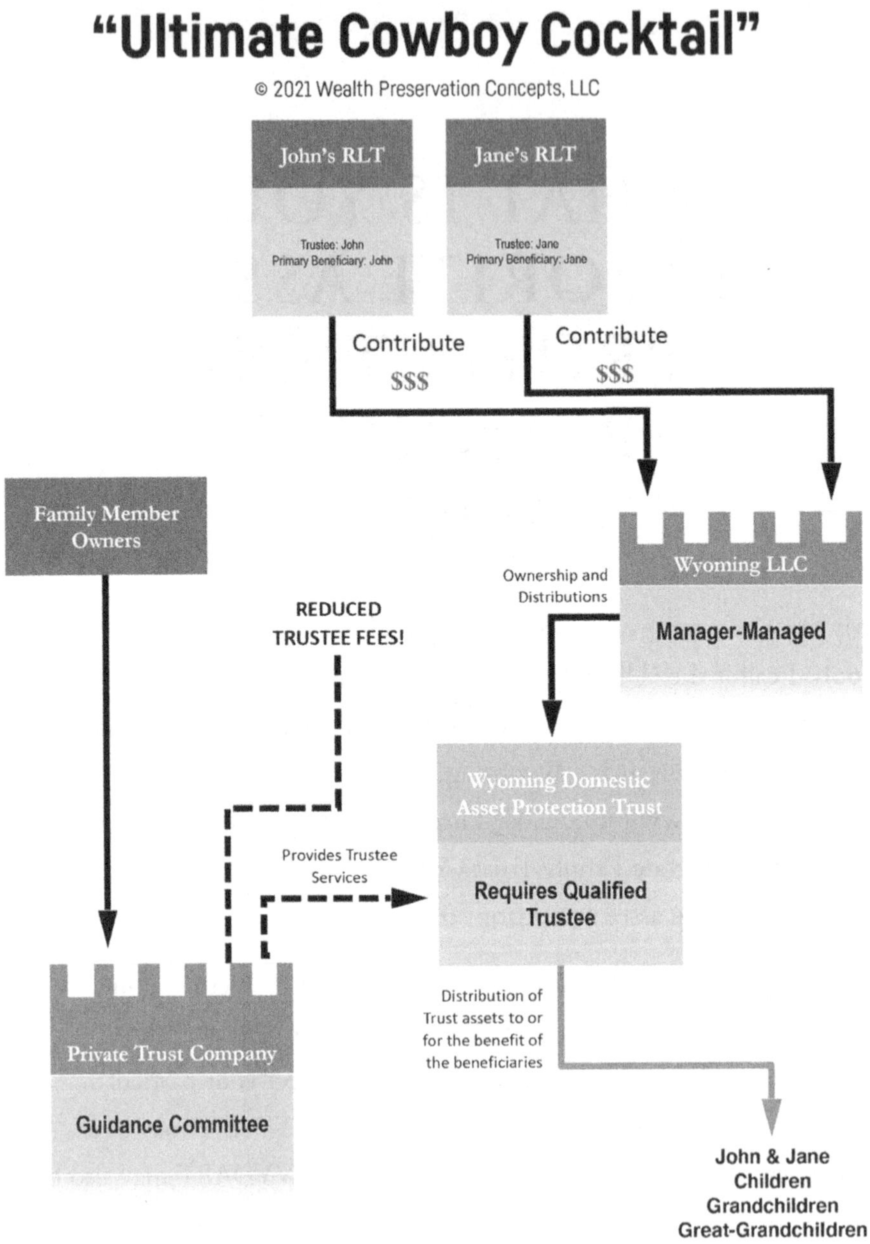
"Ultimate Cowboy Cocktail"
© 2021 Wealth Preservation Concepts, LLC
John's RLT
Trustee: John
Primary Beneficiary: John
Jane's RLT
Trustee: Jane
Primary Beneficiary: Jane
Contribute
$$$
Contribute
$$$
Family Member Owners
Wyoming LLC
Manager-Managed
Ownership and Distributions
REDUCED TRUSTEE FEES!
Wyoming Domestic Asset Protection Trust
Requires Qualified Trustee
Provides Trustee Services
Private Trust Company
Guidance Committee
Distribution of Trust assets to or for the benefit of the beneficiaries
John & Jane
Children
Grandchildren
Great-Grandchildren

and could squander all their inheritance. So, a WYDAPT beneficiary could be the trust creator or the trust creator's heirs.

The second part of the "Ultimate Cowboy Cocktail" is the LLC, which is a Wyoming Close Limited Liability Company. The Wyoming LLC offers limited liability for its members and the management. Treasured family assets are contributed to the LLC then the LLC is assigned to the WYDAPT. When combined like this, any income generated by the LLC goes directly to the WYDAPT. This "one-two punch" protects the treasured family assets from creditors and predators of beneficiaries whether the trust creator or the trust creator's heirs are the beneficiary. This combination of the LLC owned by the WYDAPT creates a significant barrier to creditors and predators. In any case, it is important that the client/beneficiary is not also the trustee.

As with any Trust you must have a qualified trustee. You can always hire an independent trust company, but I prefer a Wyoming "Private Family Trust Company" (PTC).

Wyoming is one of only a minority of states where families may choose between a self-regulated private trust company (in statutory terms a "Private Family Trust Company") or a regulated private trust company (a "Chartered Family Trust Company"). The distinction between entities is set forth in WY Stat. §13-5-301. Both entities are explicitly authorized by statue.

I prefer the self-regulated PTC as it is a self-governed entity, primarily subject to conventional fiduciary rules and the duties and powers set forth in the PTC governing documents as controlled by the directors or managers. There are limited startup costs and there are no required minimum capital requirements which makes the self-regulated PTC very attractive.

The advantages of PTCs are now far-ranging; they are no longer reserved for families with multi-generational wealth measuring in the hundreds of millions of dollars. For families who seek an alternative solution to individual or corporate trustees, the Wyoming PTC creates flexibility and shores up the Ultimate Cowboy Cocktail to protect treasured family assets.

APPENDIX E

LEGAL AUDIT CHECKLIST

DESCRIPTION	LAST REVISED	OR	DATE REVIEWED
1 Partnership or LLC Agreement	______		______
2 Corporate Documents	______		______
- Articles of incorporation	______		______
- Bylaws	______		______
- Minutes	______		______
- Wage continuation plan	______		______
- Medical reimbursement plan	______		______
- Stock certificates	______		______
- Subchapter Selection	______		______

DESCRIPTION	LAST REVISED	OR	DATE REVIEWED
3 Estate Plan	____________		____________
4 Vendor Contracts	____________		____________
5 Insurance coverage	____________		____________
6 Liability, PUP, Life,	____________		____________
7 Health, Disability	____________		____________
8 Retirement plans	____________		____________
9 Finance and Investment	____________		____________
10 Plans	____________		____________
11 Tax Returns	____________		____________
12 Marketing and Growth Plans	____________		____________
13 Employee Incentive Plans	____________		____________

FREE STUFF!!

DO YOU WANT TO KNOW HOW TO AVOID PROBATE?

Want to find out specific steps you can take to create the best plan?

What do find out how to kill Darth Vadar (IRS)?

Would you like some practical advice about how to go about this entire process?

Subscribe to Our Newsletter

These are just some of the topics that are covered 12 times a year in our free newsletter sent directly to your email inbox. We strongly believe most legal problems could be avoided if business owners had a better general knowledge about the entire legal system, planned on a regular basis to avoid problems, and involve their lawyer in their business as a regular advisor.

If you subscribe and later feel like you're wasting your time you can unsubscribe anytime. Don't worry, we promise this is not the boring "canned" newsletter that most law firms merely buy and slap their name on the form. We write it, and we aim to compel people to pay more attention to their affairs and act in their own best interest.

Free Resources

There is absolutely no cost or obligation for you to go to our website, browse around, and download or request any of the free reports, white papers, or books. You can watch the webinar at the bottom of the page under the workshops button entitled, *"The Empowered Wealth Protection Plan."*

It's pretty easy. Just go to the website, and fill out the interactive contact form that you'll find there and ask for whatever helper information you'd like to receive. We would be both excited and happy to help you.

All the best,

Jamie Moore
james@lojm.net
www.lojm.net

Randall Borkus
rhb@borkuslaw.com
www.borkuslaw.com

"One day Son all this will be yours."

Notes

Notes

Made in the USA
Monee, IL
04 November 2026

67382846R00095